DIGITAL
BODY
NEW
MEDIA
ART
2018

CICA
PRESS

DIGITAL BODY:
NEW MEDIA ART 2018

EDITOR-IN-CHIEF / ART DIRECTOR
Leejin Kim 김리진

EDITOR / DESIGNER
Heewon Bae 배희원

EDITOR
In Hye Seo 서인혜

TRANSLATORS
Doohyun Lee 이두현
Insil Choi 최인실
Minyoung Lee 이민영
Hyunju Kim 김현주

REPORTER
Choi A Rah 최아라

John Mutter, *Jo Passed 01* (2015)

FEATURED ARTISTS

Justyna Adamczyk

Maryamsadat Amirvaghefi

Alfredo Ardia

Whitney Bandel

D S Chapman

Pierre Chaumont

Jessica Dolence

Ben Ehrmann

Kun Fang

Eona Jiawei Gao

Inbar Hagai

Mary Hanlon

Maggie Hazen

Peter Hriso

Morgan Jenks

Daniel Johnson

Kevin H. Jones

Norman Klein & Margo Bistis

Alyona Larionova

Gili Lavy

Justin Lincoln

Wayne Madsen

Kushtrim Mehmeti

Tracy Miller-Robbins

John Mutter

Vasilios Papaioannu

Mikey Peterson

Pat Reynolds

Mike Richison

Anatoly Rudakov

Elissavet Sfyri

Matt Sheridan

S/N (Jennida Chase and Hassan Pitts)

Christian Tablazon

Kamil Tatara

Jessica Tsang

Leah Uchitel

Jeffrey Yip

Taylor Yocom

Kay Yoon

Liliya Zalevskaya

CONTENTS

Kushtrim Mehmeti, *Man on Cross-book*

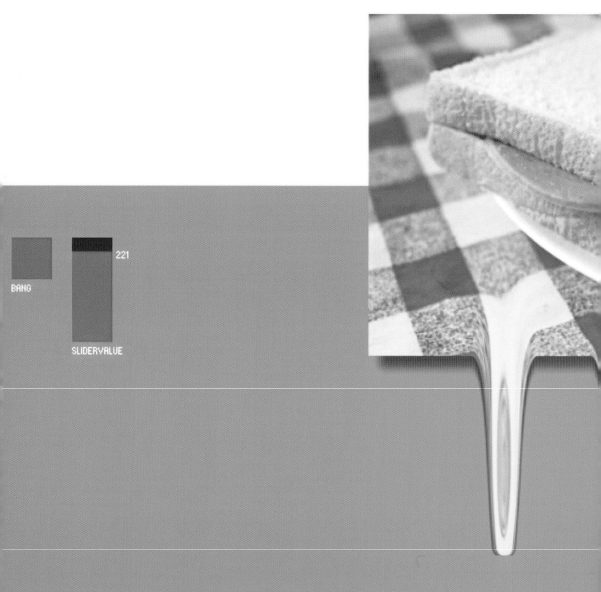

129.16

BANG

221

SLIDERVALUE

INTRO

by Leejin Kim 김리진

Artists' works and thoughts always make me ponder the subject matters, appreciate and celebrate life on a deeper level. Like a constellation in the sky, artists unfold each of their universe once I quietly look into the glimmers in the dark. *Digital Body: New Media Art 2018* features 43 new media artists worldwide who passionately represent and symbolize each of their own realities. I hope our readers plunge into the artists' worlds and celebrate the new culture in this digital era.

아티스트들을 접하면 접할수록 그 깊이감에 감탄한다. 그들의 작품과 생각들을 접하며 나는 삶을 보다 깊이 음미하는 법을 배웠다. 밤하늘에 무수한 별처럼, 적막 속에서 작은 빛을 가만히 바라볼 때 비로소 그들은 그들의 세계를 연다. *디지털 바디: 뉴 미디어 아트 2018*은 43명의 전 세계 뉴 미디어 아티스트들의 작품 세계를 소개한다. 그들은 각자의 현실을 열정적으로 재현해내고 상징화한다. 독자가 아티스트들 각자의 고유의 세계를 접하며 디지털 시대의 새로운 문화를 향유하는 장이 되었으면 한다.

Kevin H. Jones, *Hanabi* (2015), still from digital video

NEW MEDIA ART: A NEW FLOW BY THE NEW

by Choi A Rah

From 3rd to 6th of August, the CICA New Media Art Conference (NMAC) was held in Gimpo, engaging new media artists around the world to share and discuss their ideas on their works. Russian documentary photographers and video artist Anatoly Rudakov and art historiean Tinatin Ghughunishvili from Munich, Germany, new media artist Pierre Chaumont from Montréal, Canada, US-based new media artists including Justin Lincoln, S/N (Jennida Chase and Hassan Pitts), and Morgan Jenks, Computer Scientist Kyungjin Yoo from University of Maryland, and Korea-based artists Kay Yoon, Onnury Oh, EZMONSTER, Seungman Park, and Heesoo Kwon participated in this event. With the excitement of this international gathering, the conference was strongly supported by the city of Gimpo itself, having invited the Deputy Mayor Hong-Gyun Lee and city officials to the opening ceremony on the first day. This conference not only intended to gather artists to develop the cultural value of Gimpo, but also allowed new media artists the opportunity to expose their presence to a larger group of audience. The participating artists presented their idea, displayed their works, and communicated by exchanging feedbacks. As a participant of this event, the freewheeling atmosphere of the conference made me wonder if it was the concept of 'New Media' that created such accessible, energetic scene.

In August 3, 2017, NMAC began with the opening ceremony that all artists, critics, and local communities were able to get to know each other with the short presentations by artists and the performance by DJ Rumexx & Keego, and J-Rascal. Then, each artists had a chance to briefly introduce the direction of their New Media works.

The artists had presentations of their works in conference sessions from the 4th to the 5th of August. The invited artists had such diverse subject matters and methods of expression: Morgan Jenks' tracing computation of the animal skulls, S/N's different film illustrations of a single persona or creature, Anatoly Rudakov's dreamy digital photography, Pierre Chaumont's playful yet historical collections, Onnury Oh's repetitive symbolism in human relations, EZMONSTER's daily inspirational funky art, Kay Yoon's present-based symbolic art, Kyungjin Yoo's interactive-multimedia projects from the University of Maryland, Seungman Park's photography of his interpretation of death, Justin Lincoln's colorful mixture of sounds, and Heesoo Kwon's fantastical illustration of an idealistic world. Each participating artists had shown his or her unique deliverance of one's own messages, or memories, to encourage the world to take a novel perspective of Art – aside from its traditional definition. The participants' enthusiasm for Art and in-depth discussions were attractive enough to make a new media layperson want to dig deeper on the topic.

Having gone through the entire conference, the CICA NMAC 2017, as an example of was a fresh and trendy experience for me gathering within artist groups or an interactive meeting between artists and the audience tends to allow a wider perspective of ideas for both sides.

photographed by Anatoly Rudakov (middle-right, middle-left, bottom-left, bottom-right)

뉴 미디어 아트가 불러올 새로운 바람

최아라

2017년 8월 3일부터 6일, 김포시의 유일한 현대 미술관인 CICA 미술관은 11명의 뉴 미디어 국내외 아티스트를 초청하여 제 1회 2017 뉴 미디어 아트 컨퍼런스 (CICA NMAC 2017)를 개최했다. 전세계 뉴 미디어 아티스트 및 지역 주민이 뉴 미디어 아트에 관해 소통하며 향유하는 장을 마련하고자 기획된 이 행사에는 독일 Munich에서 온 러시아 다큐멘터리 사진 및 영상 작가 Anatoly Rudakov, 미술 평론가 Tinatin Ghughunishvili, 캐나다 몬트리올에서 온 뉴 미디어 아티스트 Pierre Chaumont, 미국 뉴 미디어 아티스트 Justin Lincoln, S/N (Jennida Chase and Hassan Pitts), and Morgan Jenks, 컴퓨터 사이언티스트 유경진, 한국 작가 Kay Yoon, 오온누리, EZMONSTER, 박승만, 권희수가 참여하였다. 김포시는 이러한 문화적 국제모임을 환영하는 의미에서 이홍균 부시장님께서 축사하셨으며 시 공무원들이 첫날의 오프닝 파티를 함께 했다. CICA NMAC 2017는 전문가 및 대중에게 뉴 미디어 아트를 소개하고, 뉴 미디어가 던지는 여러 가지 철학적, 문화적 의미와 이슈들에 대해 생각해보고 서로 의견을 나눔을 통해 문화적 가치를 형성해 나아고자 기획되었다. 컨퍼런스는 첫날 오프닝 파티를 시작으로, 이틀간 작가들의 작품 전시 및 상호적 비평, 토론 시간을 갖고, 김포시 문화 사업 현장 방문, 마지막 날에 굿바이 브런치 및 퍼포먼스로 마무리 지어졌다.

현대미술이 시대의 흐름에 따라 변해가고 있는 만큼, 예술의 정의 또한 한층 넓어진 범위를 품게 되었다. 예술작품은 더 이상 관람자와 작가 간의 일방적인 소통으로 '감상'되기만 하는 것이 아닌, 상호적 교류로 관객의 참여를 유도하며, 작품과의 거리를 그대로 유지하기도, 한없이 좁혀서 관람자를 작품의 일부로 느껴지게도 하게 되었다. 뉴 미디어 아트는, 기술적 발전과 예술의 결합을 시발점으로 사람들이 '예술'이라는 분야를 너무 먼 세상 이야기로 느껴지는 것을 줄여나가고 있다. 과거 예술이 부유층, 혹은 특권층만의 부산물로 여겨졌던 데에는, 예술 작품의 가치가 원본성과 현존성과 같이 특수하고 한정된 시공간이라는 조건을 요구했기 때문이다. 하지만 지금은 기술의 발달로 수많은 예술 작품들이 레플리카, 재현물, 온라인 파일 등으로 누구나 어렵지 않게 접할 수 있는 상태가 되었다. 혹자는 이러한 높은 접근성이 과거 예술이 갖던 본연의 '아우라'를 침해한다고 주장한다. 하지만 필자는 예술이 고고하고 고독한 특권층의 영역으로만 남는다면, 그 또한 작품 본연의 가치를 드러낼 수 없을 것으고 생각한다.

신진 뉴 미디어 아트 작가들을 위해 기획된 이번 콘퍼런스는, 작가들이 서로의 작품들을 다른 시각에서 바라볼 수 있는, 더 많은 사람에게 자신의 존재와 작품 세계를 선보일 기회였을 것이다. 세미나를 진행하며, 같은 뉴 미디어 아트를 다루는 11명의 작가가 다양한 개념을 가지고 작업을 하고, 서로의 작품을 완전히 다른 시각으로 볼 수 있다는 점에서 매우 흥미로운 시간이었다. 그들은 같은 분야에 속해있으면서도, 서로의 의견을 마주하고 갈등을 겪으며 더 넓고 다양한 생각을 하게 된 것 같았다. 언젠가 예술이 '어려운 문화생활'이라는 관념을 벗어나서 모두의 생활 속에서 예술을 발견할 수 있게 되는 날이 온다면, 우리는 얼마나 더 새로운 세상을 마주하게 될지 기대되는 바이다.

PIERRE CHAUMONT

Pierre Chaumont, *All This For Brioche (Marie-Antoinette)* (2016) (left), *Breaking The Spell (Perseus Beheading Medusa)* (2016) (center)

Pierre Chaumont, *Power Comes With Feet Of Clay (Louis XIV)* (2015) (right)

The destruction of world heritage sites and artworks in Mosul, Iraq, in February 2015, sparked a global move to digitize and preserve important works and monuments. Institutions and individuals were called upon to create, refine and disseminate digital scans of the lost works of art. The months following the attacks, we witness the emergence of initiatives such as Rekrei (formaly known as project Mosul) or Scan The World emerge that would solely focus on building this archive. By being available to anyone having access to a computer and Internet, a fundamental shift operated which is reshaping our relation towards Art and how we experience it.

This process is transforming where we experience Art, as every scanned object is now accessible regardless of location, wealth or ownership. Previously bound to cultural institutions, the digital archive is now easily obtainable to viewers and can be manipulated, collected, and modified free of decorum. In a way it transposes the museum into the computer, peels off all our preconceived behaviours toward the object, while granting us new powers on the works by allowing us to interact with the files.

Because these 3D files are the visible layers taken invisibly and directly from the initial artwork or monument, they hold the same cultural value as the physical work. We can easily affirm this because materiality and uniqueness are notions anchored in the art market rather than art history. The fact that The Thinker of Rodin is an edition of 2 or 35, or a preparatory plaster cast rather than the bronze version has little to do with the cultural impact of the artwork itself.

Also, it is not unusual to learn about the greatness of lost works of art through photographs. The cultural value is found in knowledge of the

Pierre Chaumont, *Goliath's Revenge* (2015)

object rather than the object itself, and materiality is just triggers the desire to obtain it. During the process of this digital translation the market value and the aura of each and every original piece is stripped away to, alternatively, leave only the history and its cultural value.

By the gathering of these 3D files, the computer progressively becomes a digital museum, and because of this, the question of the cultural value arises. If the museum is the place where artworks rest for eternity as Adorno said, the digital one allows to reconsider conceptually and aesthetically these masterpieces by putting them through a 3D program. The malleability of the scans generates a paradigm shift; these cultural objects become materials that can be rethought and reassessed, actualizing how we learned to memorize them. The archive therefore carries a dual function; on one side, when collected, it turns into a digital mausoleum, where its physicality is put in relation with the knowledge we made of it until now. It is approached in the same way as an encyclopaedia ; taking each object as a visual reference to the whole art historical knowledge. But on the other side, by putting it through a 3D program, it then develops into a conceptually porous substance that allows us to insert new contexts and new ways of seeing. In a sense, it reignites the discussions about the works by introducing a gap with the original, therefore putting it in a liberated and experimental zone. The institutions have "the power to interpret the archive" as Derrida mentioned, but as soon as the file is downloaded and activated by the viewer, artist or historian, they in turn become the interpreters.

Moreover, Derrida points out in Archive Fever that "There is no political power without a control of the archive, if not memory." This led me to search for who or which institutions were behind this initiative and/or providing scans. I then quickly discovered that even though it started as a way to counter the destruction that happened in Mosul, it rapidly switched emphasis on another geographical history by its own institutions: the Western ones. The destroyed winged lion of Mosul became surrounded by busts of christian cardinals, western allegories of love and second world war monuments. That historical focus pushed by museums such as the Louvre, the V&A, the Met or the British Museum concentrates the accessibility and the production of these 3d files to their own collections. Preserving then becomes the privilege of the hegemony; where technology-advanced countries get to define,choose and provide cultural material for the rest of the world. From this stems a cultural colonialism; relegated to the background, non-western artworks are drowned in western ideals. Moreover, it not only emphasizes Eurocentric views on conservation and History, as the explanation given on each piece is mediated by the institution itself, but also impoverishes the discourse on non-western artworks, because of the lack of perspective from the community. This leaves viewers to interact with the pieces on a purely visual facet, which unconsciously erases deeper cultural meanings.

Impoverishment of History and meaning is obviously present with non-western artworks, but it also happens (less often though) with Occidental pieces. Because viewers judge a work to collect primarily from its aesthetic qualities, they might gather files that perpetuate a colonialist perspective. To give you an example we will take the file of Sir Henry Havelock. The original work is a monument found on Trafalgar Square and was erected in 1861 to commemorate the general's accomplishment in recapturing certain cities during the Indian "Mutiny" of 1857. Knowing this and the important colonial past of England, contemporary viewers cannot feel anything but unease when they find out that this sculpture was included in the archive to be disseminated. But to feel that uneasiness, you need a deeper research on the original or at least a more expanded history that includes the vision of the "Other" within the artwork to counter this cycle. Else, you share and use a contentious material.

The 3D archive is a fascinating double-edged sword. It questions anew our vision of the museum, our experience with Art, and the way we collect in the digital era. Unfortunately, it can also be a tool for cultural hegemony and where Historical facts are erased or forgotten to the benefit of the institution producing it, henceforth reinforcing the gap between cultures. Finally, as we mentioned earlier, for the archive to be an effective counter measure to cultural biases, it falls into the collectors hand to make an enlightened choice. Only by going beyond the visual aspect of these files that we can create new meanings and point of views; the image is only the first step to highlight a deeper system of Power.

2015년 2월 이라크의 모술에서 세계문화유산과 예술품들이 파괴된 사건 이후, 중요한 작품과 기념물을 디지털화하고 보존하자는 전 세계적인 움직임이 확산되었다. 이와 관련된 기관들과 사람들은 잃어버린 예술 작품들을 디지털 스캔으로 구현하고 다듬어서 전파하는 작업을 실행했다. 모술 사태가 일어난 후 수개월 동안, 이전에 "모술 프로젝트"라 불렸던 Rekrei나 "스캔 더 월드"와 같이 오직 아카이브 구축에 집중하는 계획들이 등장했다. 컴퓨터와 인터넷을 사용하는 모든 사람이 이 아카이브에 접근할 수 있다는 점에서, 예술과 우리의 관계와 우리가 이것을 경험하는 방법을 재형성하는 근본적인 변화가 일어났다.

이러한 과정을 통해 장소나 부유한 정도, 그리고 소유권과 상관없이 우리가 스캔한 모든 작업에 접근이 가능해지면서 우리가 어디서 예술을 경험하는지에 변화가 왔다. 이전까지 문화기관에서나 볼 수 있던 작품들을 이제 우리는 디지털 아카이브로 얻을 수 있게 되었고, 그것들을 아무 거리낌 없이 조작하고, 수집하고, 수정한다. 어떤 면에서 디지털 아카이빙은 미술관을 컴퓨터 안에 옮겨놓은 것이다. 그리고 오랫동안 자리 잡은 사물을 대하는 우리의 태도에서 탈피하게 하며, 자료들과 교류하는 것을 허용함으로써 우리에게 작품들에 대한 권력을 부여한다.

이러한 3D 자료들은 원래의 예술작품이나 모뉴먼트로부터 직접 도출한 가시적인 층이기 때문에, 그것들은 실제 작품과 동일한 문화적 가치를 갖고 있다. 물질성과 고유함은 미술사보다는 시장에 기반을 둔 개념이기 때문이다. 이를테면 로댕의 〈생각하는 사람〉이 35개의 에디션 중 두 번째이며, 브론즈가 아닌 석고의 사전 모형이라는 사실은 작품 자체가 가지고 있는 문화적 영향과 큰 상관이 없다.

또한, 사진을 통해 잃어버린 예술작품의 위대함에 대해 배우는 것은 일반적이다. 작품의 문화적 가치는 작품 자체가 아니라 작품과 관련한 지식에서 발견되며, 물질성이 이것을 얻고자 하는 욕망을 자극하는 것이다. 이러한 디지털 번역 과정이 진행되는 동안 모든 각각의 원본 작품이 가진 시장적 가치와 아우라가 벗겨지면서 그 자리에는 이의 역사와 문화적 가치만이 남는다.

이 3D 자료들이 모여 컴퓨터는 점차 디지털 박물관이 되는데, 이는 문화적 가치에 대한 의문을 갖게 한다. 아도르노가 말한 것처럼 미술관이 예술품이 영원히 안식하는 장소라면, 디지털 미술관은 3D 프로그램을 통해 명작들을 그 안에 넣음으로써 작품에 대한 개념적이고 미학적으로 재고하게 한다. 작품의 스캔본이 가진 유연성은

Pierre Chaumont, *When The Laurels Wither (Sir Henry Havelock)* (2016)

패러다임에 변화를 가져온다. 이 문화적 대상은 우리가 다시 생각하고 재평가할 수 있는 자료가 되어 우리가 예술품들을 암기하도록 배운 방법을 실현하였다. 따라서 아카이브는 이중의 기능을 가진다. 한편으로, 아카이브는 수집되면서 우리가 지금까지 그것을 이용해 만든 지식과 관련한 물질성을 쌓아 두는 디지털 묘지로 바뀐다. 이는 백과사전과 같은 방식을 취하는데, 각 대상을 미술사적 지식 전체에 대한 시각적 참고로 삼는다는 점에서 그렇다. 그러나 다른 한편으로는, 3D 프로그램을 통해 자료를 집어넣으면서 아카이브에 개념적으로 통과할 수 있는 구멍이 생기고, 이는 우리가 새로운 맥락이나 바라보는 새로운 방법을 추가할 수 있게 한다. 어떤 면에서는, 원본과의 간격을 드러내 보이며 작품에 대한 토론을 재개시키고, 결국 이를 해방되고 실험적인 구역에 놓는다. 데리다가 언급한 것처럼 교육기관은 "아카이브를 해석할 수 있는 권위"를 가지고 있지만, 보는 이, 아티스트 또는 역사가가 자료를 다운로드하여 활용하는 순간 그들도 곧 해석자가 된다.

또한, 데리다는 본인의 책 『아카이브 열병 Archive Fever』에서 "기억까지는 아니더라도 아카이브의 통제가 없는 정치적 권력은 없다"라고 강조했다. 이는 내가 디지털화 계획과 스캔본을 제공하는 배후에 어떤 이들과 기관들이 있는지 찾아보게 했다. 나는 이것이 미술에서 발생한 파괴에 대응하기 위한 방법으로 시작했음에도 불구하고, 빠르게 서구의 지리적 역사로 그 강조가 변환되었다는 사실을 발견했다. 파괴된 모술의 날개 달린 사자는 크리스챤 추기경의 흉상과 사랑에 대한 서구의 우화들, 세계 2차 대전 기념비로 둘러싸여 있다. 루브르 박물관, 빅토리아 앤드 알버트 미술관, 메트로폴리탄 미술관 혹은 대영 박물관과 같은 문화 기관이 추진한 역사적인 초점은 그들의 콜렉션들을 3D 자료로 제작하는 것과 그것들에 대한 접근성에 집중되었다. 이러한 3D 파일의 접근성과 제작을 자신의 소장품에 집중한다. 그리하면 기술 선진국들이 전 세계의 문화 자료를 정의하고 선택하고 제공하게 되면서 보존은 곧 헤게모니의 특권이 된다. 여기서 바로 배경으로 밀려난 비서구권의 예술품이 서구의 이상에 익사하는 문화적 식민주의가 발생한다. 더 나아가, 각 작품에 대한 설명이 기관 자체에서 중재되기 때문에 보존과 역사에 대한 유럽 중심적 시각을 강조할 뿐만 아니라, 비서구권의 예술 작품에 대한 담론을 빈약하게 한다. 이는 비서구권 사회의 관점이 부족하기 때문이다. 이는 보는 이가 작품들과 오직 시각적인 측면에서 소통하게 하며, 무의식적으로 작품의 더 깊은 문화적 의미를 제거하게 한다.

역사와 의미의 빈곤은 비서구권의 작품들에 당연히 존재하는 것이지만, 이것은 종종 서구의 작품들에서도 발생한다. 보는 이들은 수집할 작품을 우선적으로 이의 미학적 성질을 통해 판단하기 때문에, 그들은 식민주의적 관점을 관통하는 자료들을 모을지도 모른다. 헨리 헤블록 경(Sir Henry Havelock)의 자료를 예로 들어보겠다. 원작은 트라팔가 광장에 1961년에 세워진 기념물로, 1857년 인도 "폭동" 기간 동안 장군이 특정 도시들을 탈환하는 데에 성공한 것을 기념하는 것이었다. 이러한 사실과 영국의 식민 역사를 아는 동시대의 보는 이들은 이 조각이 아카이브에 포함되어 널리 전파된다는 것을 알았을 때 불편함 밖에 느낄 수 없다. 그러나 그런 불편함을 느끼려면 원본에 대한 더 깊은 연구를 하거나, 반박하기 위해서 적어도 그 작품에 내포된 "타자"의 시점을 포함하는 더 확장된 역사에 대해 공부할 필요가 있다. 이 연구에는 이 주기에 대응하는 예술 작품 내의 "기타"라는 버전이 포함된다. 그렇지 않으면, 논쟁의 여지가 있는 자료를 공유하고 사용하는 것이다.

3D 아카이브는 매력적인 양날의 검이다. 이는 디지털 시대를 사는 우리의 박물관에 대한 비전, 예술에 대한 경험, 그리고 수집하는 방식에 대해 새로운 질문을 던진다. 안타깝게도 이는 문화적 헤게모니를 위한 도구일 수도 있고, 역사적인 사실들이 기관의 이익을 위해 지워지거나 잊히는 곳일 수도 있으며, 이후에 문화 간의 격차를 더 벌어지게 할 수 있다. 마지막으로, 앞에서 언급했듯이, 아카이브가 문화적 편향에 대한 효과적인 대응책이 되려면, 그것은 깨우친 선택을 하는 수집가의 손에 달렸다. 오직 자료의 시각적 측면을 넘어섬으로써 새로운 의미와 관점을 창출할 수 있다. 이미지는 더 깊은 권력의 체계를 강조하는 첫걸음일 뿐이다.

Pierre Chaumont was born in 1987 in Libourne(France): he lives and works in Montréal (Canada). He spends his time between Montréal and Tokyo. His artworks were shown in United States, China, Japan, Greece, Slovenia and Canada. He is part of the collection of the Museum of Contemporary Art in Laurentians, The Museum of Art in Lendava, Slovenia, the Loto-Quebec Collection, the New Ark Library collection and in many private collections.

Pierre Chaumont는 1987년 프랑스 Libourne 에서 태어났으며, 캐나다 몬트리올에서 살면서 일하고 있다. 그는 몬트리올과 도쿄에서 시간을 보내곤 한다. 그의 작품은 미국, 중국, 일본, 그리스, 슬로베니아 및 캐나다에서 전시되었으며 Laurentians의 현대 미술관, 슬로베니아 Lendava의 미술관, Loto-Quebec 컬렉션, 뉴악 도서관 컬렉션 등 다수의 개인 컬렉터들에게 소장되어 있다.

JUSTIN LINCOLN

Artist as Noise Source

"Cage and Rauschenberg offered up a view of artistic practice as a leveled collaboration among artist, audience, and materials. At another level, though, their work echoed and ultimately celebrated a migration toward the decentralized, systems-oriented forms of thought then occurring at the center of the scientific establishment.

…for them, the making of art had become the building of systems of pattern and randomness, and thus, in Claude Shannon's sense, of information." (Turner, 47)

In much the same way that Claude Shannon's theories of Information Science were a common frame of reference for John Cage, Robert Rauschenberg, Nam Jun Paik, and certain other mid to late 20th century artists; they have also become for me enduring points of fascination. In particular Shannon's Mathematical Theory of Communication, which was developed to help Bell Laboratories solve problems in long distance telecommunication, has helped me re-think and re-define my own role as artist.

https://en.wikipedia.org/wiki/A_ Mathematical_Theory_of_Communication

Please see my own modified version (included in the materials sent here) printed below. My own sleight adjustments to Shannon's model from 1949 come from a re-thinking of the artists place in systems of communication.

At one point in my life I would have placed the artist in the role of information source, which parallels the primary role of a person placing a long distance call and speaking into the receiver of their phone. Some artists today may still claim that role. However, I believe that we are now so awash in cultural/ media messages that it is important for some artists to act as noise which interferes, modifies, and ultimately slows down the reception of those messages for their ultimate destination, the audience. In Shannon's model that destination might be the person listening on the other end of the telephone line.

In Shannon's model noise is a disruptive problem in communication that can never ultimately be wiped out. One is left with Information Science's famous "signal to noise ratio." I believe that my role, and the role of many contemporary digital artists is to adjust that ratio in different media environments and to invite contemplation and questioning of the ways that they become control mechanisms for our (sub)consciousness. Artists can and should be disruptive. They should embrace noise, ambiguity, distortion, and misdirection. They should fight any dream of pure, sanitized, or noiseless communication. They should feel free to re-arrange linear thinking. They should highlight the speeds and flows of information to call attention to the forms as well as content in our media environments.

Now of course, due to the advent of personal computing, the internet, Web 2.0, and cellphone technology one might see Shannon's diagram as being limited due to its illustration of a one way flow of information. Concurrent with Shannon's model other scientists like Norbert Weiner and Warren Weaver were developing and disseminating ideas of cybernetics and feedback loops. Obviously, even in the days of analog telephony, the two parties in a phone conversation could easily switch roles in terms of Source and Destination.

More importantly though, the coupling of humans with machines to facilitate communication absolutely alters those communications. That coupling is laid bare in Shannon's deceptively simple diagram. In our contemporary culture we may often sing the praises of technological progress or bemoan a bygone era in which life seemed to flow at a more simple and steady pace. However we have very little clear headed analysis of how our latest communication devices are shaping our perceptions or the way that our perceptions in turn get fed back into the development of the next gadgets being marketed back to us.

Once any image, sound, or text is brought into

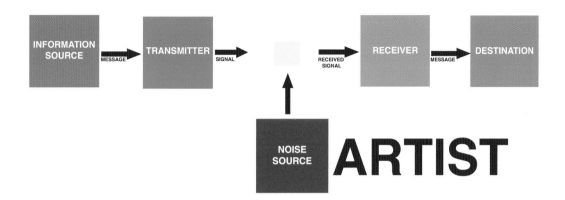

our computers it is basically data. Shannon's Mathematical Model went on to suggest that data could be measured in units referred to as bits. For an engineer these bits are basically neutral in terms of meaning as they pass from transmitter to receiver . The information, or combination of bits, is generally meaningful for the Source or Destination but one might argue that even that isn't always the case. Following along the lines of Information Science I often suggest to my students that "Meaning is simply when a collection of facts give us feelings. " Whether those facts are a bunch of statistics or a painting on a wall, if we don't feel anything those facts are basically meaningless to us. Adding noise to data is a way to alter the meaning of data.

As artists, in the end, meaning matters to us....but as we make our work we often hold meaning in suspension as the signal of bits or analog information passes through the lines of art production.

In terms of production, over the last decade or so I have gotten increasingly involved in creative computer programming and audio/video synthesis. At the root of both programming and synthesis is an impulse to play with noise.....to alter, distort, and re-contextualize the images and sounds that seem to inundate my attention.

The bug-a-boos of copyright and it's blurry boundaries of fair use sometimes provoke some anxiety for me. I am constantly and consistently making my work out of work by countless other people that came before me. I worry am I being lazy or ethically suspect. But then again, I know how consumed I am with my work, how exhaustive and exhausting it can be to make it, and how meaningful that work has become for me. That is not to say that it will be meaningful for mass audiences today. Perhaps as Paul Klee said, the true artist makes work for an audience yet to come. Perhaps it is a kind of existential gamble. Better yet, I like to think of it as part of a larger conversation amongst creators past, present, and future.

It can be humbling as an artist and programmer to keep myself out of the role of information source when making my work, to be mindful of my primary role as noise source. Meanwhile, simply being a noise source makes me question myself whenever temporarily taking on any mantle of authority in art making or academia. It can make me feel marginal or illegible even inside discourses in which I contribute...but it is also sometimes a great deal of fun.

Cited

From Counterculture to CyberCulture : Stewart Brand, the Whole Earth Network, and the Rise of Digital Utopianism. Fred Turner. The University of Chicago Press. 2006.

아티스트로서의 노이즈 소스

"케이지와 라우센버그는 예술적 실천에 대해 예술가, 청중 및 자료 간의 동등한 협업이라는 견해를 제시했다. 그러나 또 다른 차원에서, 그들의 작업은 탈중심화되고 시스템 지향적인 생각의 형태들도 이동하여 후에 과학적 시설의 중심에서 발생하는 것에 메아리쳤으며 결국 그것을 기념했다.

... 그들에게 예술을 만드는 것은 패턴과 무작위성의 체계를 구축하는 것이 되었고, 이것은, 클라우드 섀넌의 개념에서, 정보를 구축하는 것을 의미한다."(터너, 47)

클라우드 섀넌의 정보 과학 이론은 백남준, 존 케이지, 로버트 라우센버그 그리고 20세기 중후기의 다른 예술가들이 언급한 것과 공통된 프레임을 나타낸다. 또한, 그들은 나에게 오랫동안 매력적인 포인트로 다가왔다. 특히 벨 실험실의 장거리 전기 통신 문제 해결을 위해 발전된 섀넌의 커뮤니케이션의 수학적 이론은, 예술가로서의 나의 역할을 재정의하고 재고하게끔 했다.

https://en.wikipedia.org/wiki/A_Mathematical_Theory_of_Communication

아래에 보이는 나의 수정된 버전을 보길 바란다. 내가 수정한 섀넌의 1949년 모델은 커뮤니케이션 시스템 안의 예술가의 위치에 관한 나의 생각을 재고한 것이다.

내 인생에서의 한 지점에서 나는 예술가가 정보원의 역할을 한다고 여겼다. 이것은 장거리 전화를 걸어서 전화기에 대고 말하는 사람의 주된 역할과 같다. 아마 몇몇 예술가들은 아마 여전히 그 역할을 주장할 것이다. 그러나 나는 우리 주변에 문화/미디어 메시지가 넘쳐나기 때문에, 몇몇 예술가 메시지의 궁극적 목적지인 청중의 수신을 방해하고, 수정하고, 궁극적으로 속도를 늦추는 소음으로 작용하는 것은 중요하다고 믿는다. 섀넌의 모델에서는 그 목적지는 전화선의 반대쪽에서 있는 사람일 것이다.

섀논의 모델에서 말하는 소음이란 궁극적으로 절대 사라질 수 없는 의사소통에서의 방해 적 문제이다. 하나는 정보과학의 유명한 "신호 대 잡음 비율"이다. 많은 동시대 디지털 예술가와 나의 역할은 다양한 미디어 환경에서 이 비율을 조정하고 그들이 우리의 (잠재) 의식을 위한 메커니즘을 제어할 수 있는 방법에 대해 숙고하고 질문하는 것이다. 아티스트는 파괴적일 수 있으며 파괴적이어야 한다. 그들은 소음, 모호함, 왜곡 및 잘못된 지시를 받아들여야 한다. 그들은 순수하고 위생적이며 소음이 없는 의사소통의 꿈에 대항해 싸워야 한다. 그들은 직선적 사고방식을 자유롭게 조정할 수

Justin Lincoln, *Wobbled Grid (2017),* still images from digital video

있어야 한다. 그들은 미디어 환경의 콘텐츠는 물론 형식에 주의를 환기하기 위한 정보의 속도와 흐름을 강조해야 한다.

물론 개인용 컴퓨터, 인터넷, Web 2.0 및 휴대폰 기술의 출현하면서 섀넌의 다이어그램은 일방적인 정보 흐름으로 인해 제한적이라고도 볼 수 있다. 섀넌의 모델과 동시에 노버트 와이너(Norbert Weiner)와 워렌 위버(Warren Weaver)와 같은 다른 과학자들은 사이버네틱스와 피드백 회로에 대한 아이디어를 개발하고 보급하고 있었다. 물론, 아날로그 전화 통신 방법을 사용하던 때에도, 전화 통화를 하는 두 사람이 원본과 대상(Source and Destination)의 개념에서 역할을 쉽게 바꿀 수 있었다.

그러나 더 중요한 점은 의사소통을 원활하게 하기 위해 사람과 기계를 연결하는 것은 그 의사소통을 완전히 바꾼다는 것이다. 그 연결은 섀넌의 너무나도 간단한 다이어그램에서 드러난다. 우리의 동시대 문화에서 우리는 종종 기술 진보에 대해 찬양하거나, 삶이 보다 간단하고 안정된 속도로 흐르던 듯했던 과거의 시대에 대해 한탄할 수도 있습니다. 그러나 우리는 최신 통신 장치가 우리의 인식에 어떻게 영향을 끼치고 있는지 또는 우리의 인식이 우리에게 판매될 다음 장치의 개발로 다시 반영되는 방식에 대한 명확한 분석을 거의 갖고 있지 않다.

우리의 컴퓨터로 옮겨진 모든 이미지, 사운드, 또는 텍스트는 기본적으로 데이터다. 섀넌의 수학적 모델은 데이터를 비트라고 하는 단위로 측정할 수 있다고 제안했다. 이 비트는 송신기에서 수신기로 전달된다는 점에 있어 엔지니어에게 기본적으로 중립적인 의미가 있다. 정보 또는 비트의 조합은 일반적으로 "원본 또는 대상"에게 의미가 있지만, 항상 그렇지 않다고 주장 할 수도 있다. 정보 과학의 길을 밟으면서 나는 종종 학생들에게 "의미는, 단순하게, 사실들이 모여서 감정을 느끼게 하는 것이다"라는 말을 한다. 그 사실들이 다수의 통계이든 벽에 걸린 그림이든 우리가 그 사실을 전혀 느끼지 못한다면 그것들은 의미가 없다. 데이터에 소음을 추가하는 것은 데이터의 의미에 변화를 주는 방법이다.

예술가로서, 의미는 결국 우리에게 중요한 것이 된다...그러나 비트의 신호나 아날로그 정보가 예술제작의 길을 통과함에 따라 우리가 작품을 만들 때 우리는 종종 의미를 미결로 남겨둔다.

제작 면에서 볼 때 지난 10년 동안 나는 창조적 컴퓨터 프로그래밍과 오디오/비디오 통합에 점점 더 관여해왔다. 프로그래밍과 통합의 근원은 내 집중을 완전히 사로잡은 듯 보이는 이미지와 소리를 바꾸고, 변형시키고, 재-문맥화하는 소음을 사용하고자 하는 충동이다.

저작권 침해와 공정한 사용의 모호한 경계는 때때로 나를 불안하게 한다. 나는 끊임없이 그리고 일관되게 나보다 먼저 산 사람들의 수많은 작업들로 나의 작업을 제작한다. 나는 혹시 내가 게으르지는 않은지 도덕적으로 의심스럽지는 않은지 걱정한다. 그러나 나는 내가 내 작업에 얼마나 소진되었는지, 이를 제작하는 것이 얼마나 철저하고 지치게 하는 일인지, 그리고 이 작업이 나에게 어떤 의미가 되었는지 알고 있다. 이것이 수많은 대중에게 의미가 있을 것이라는 뜻이 아니다. 파울 클레가 말했듯 진정한 예술가는 미래의 관객을 위해 작품을 만드는 자일 수 있다. 그것은 아마 일종의 실존적인 도박일 것이다. 더 좋게는, 나는 이것을 과거, 현재, 미래의 창작자들 간의 대화의 일부로 생각하고 싶다.

예술가와 프로그래머로서 내 작업을 할 때 스스로 정보원으로서의 역할에서 벗어나, 나의 주된 역할은 소음원이라는 것을 유념하는 것은 겸손하다고 할 수 있다. 한편, 단순히 소음원이 되는 것은 예술 제작이나 학계에서 일시적으로 지휘의 역할을 할 때마다 스스로에게 의문을 갖게 된다. 이는 심지어 내가 기여하는 담론 안에서 내가 주변부에 있거나 눈에 띄지 않는다고 느끼게 만든다... 그러나 이것은 또한 때때로 제법 재밌기도 하다.

Justin Lincoln is an experimental artist and educator who teaches New Genres & Digital Art at Whitman College in Walla Walla, Washington. His work involves creative computer programming, the online community of tumblr, video montage, and the history of experimental film. He is a prolific presence online and his work shows extensively in international exhibitions and screenings. Recent screenings include The Chicago Underground Film Festival, FILE Digital Languages Festival in Sao Paulo, Brazil, the Dallas VideoFest, and the Punto Y Raya Festival in Karlruhe, Germany. Lately he has been getting lost in the sounds of his OP-1 synthesizer.

저스틴 링컨은 실험적인 예술가이자 교육자로 워싱턴주 알라왈라 소재의 휘트먼 대학에서 새로운 장르와 디지털 아트를 가르친다. 그의 작품은 창의적인 컴퓨터 프로그래밍과 텀블러의 온라인 커뮤니티, 비디오 몽타주 및 실험영화의 역사를 주요 요소로 수반한다. 그는 온라인에 다작을 올리며 그의 작품은 국제전시회 및 상영회에 광범위하게 전시된다. 최근 상영은 시카고 언더그라운드 영화제, 브라질 상파울루 FILE Digital Languages Festival, the Dallas VideoFest 그리고 독일 칼츄에 the Punto Y Raya Festival에 널리 상영되었다. 후에 그는 OP-1 신시사이저 소리에 푹 빠져 길을 잃었다.

MORGAN JENKS

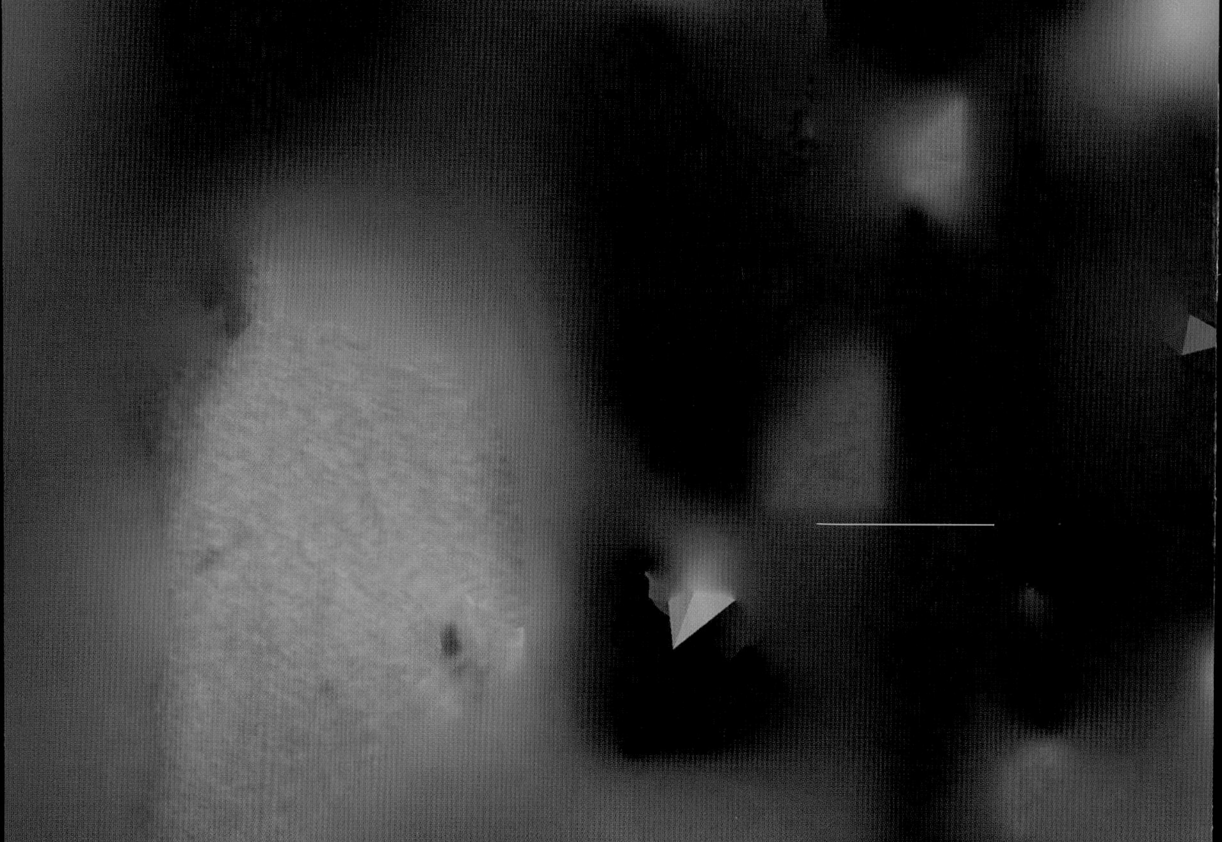

Skull Spool

by Morgan Jenks

Hacked 3D scanning software picks through the geometry of an animal skull in wandering paths reminiscent of insects, generating ghostly reconfigurations with nuanced details.

These pieces branched from other process based work where I was exploring wild landscapes and capturing imagery of vegetation to create 3D models using photogrammetry, a technique which combines photographs from different angles of a subject to triangulate the surface contours. I crafted algorithms to crawl across the organic geometry of these scans using proximity to lead the way, thinking about how plants might feel themselves. On one trip, I came across a coyote skull in the woods. I was immediately struck by a depth of empathy. Whereas the forms of plants are engaging to me in an sense of wonder and architectural otherness, the skull was personally relatable. The fixation of gazing into its eyes got me thinking about the growth and mortality of our animal bodies, a sense of instinctive alarm, and the tetheredness we have to matter. I took the skull home and began to experiment with ways of abstracting it, manually editing small images of faces into the photographs of the skull which produce aberrant 3D geometry and running the geometric unravelling through facial recognition to target areas for vertex displacement.

I feel that lots of issues humanity faces with the environment and with artificial intelligence stem from a feeling of dissociation, isolated identity where reality is actually intertwined. Will technology save us from death? Will we become extinct? If not, then what? Perhaps these pieces can help to crack open these questions.

Morgan Jenks, *The Entire SkullSpool Image Series* (2017)

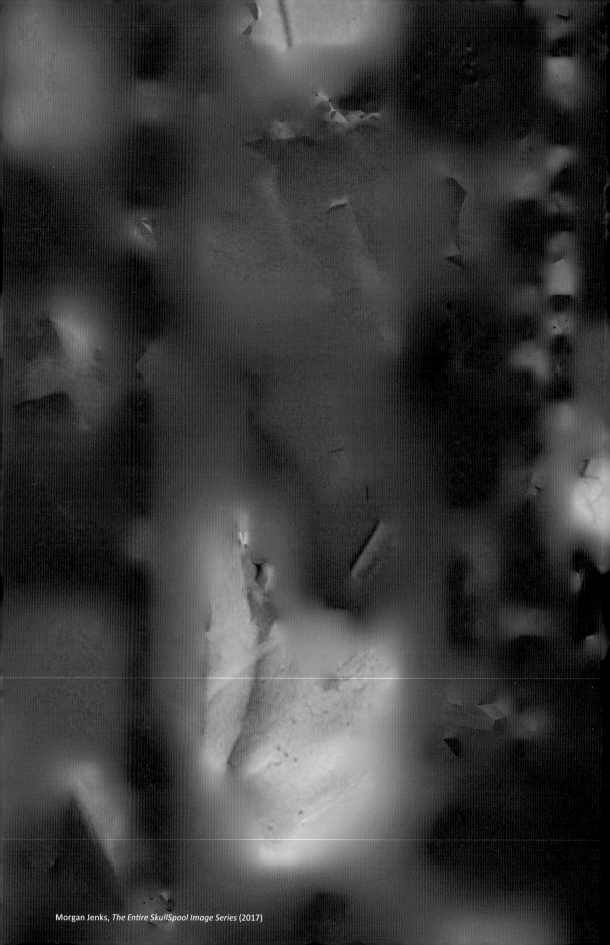

Morgan Jenks, *The Entire SkullSpool Image Series* (2017)

두개골 스풀

Morgan Jenks

해킹된 3D 스캐닝 소프트웨어는 방황하는 길에서 동물 두개골의 기하학을 통해 곤충을 연상시키는 뉘앙스가 있는 재구성을 조용히 일으킨다.

이전 프로세스 기반 작업에서 파생된 이 작품은 작가 본인이 야생 풍경을 탐험하고 식물 사진의 이미지를 캡처해 3D 모델을 만들기 위한 사진 측량법을 사용했다. 여기에 사용된 기술은 피사체의 다른 각도에서 찍은 사진을 결합해 표면 윤곽을 삼각화하는 기술이다. 한 여행 중, 나는 숲에서 코요태 두개골을 발견했다. 나는 즉시 깊은 감정 이입에 치달았다. 식물의 형태가 나에게 경이로움과 건축적 이질감이란 의미였지만, 두개골은 나에게 개인적인 관계가 있었다. 두개골의 눈에 집중해 응시하면 사체의 성장과 사망, 본능적인 감각이 주는 경보, 그리고 우리가 중요하게 여기는 얽매임에 대해 생각하게 했다. 나는 그 두개골을 집으로 가져와 이를 추상화할 방법을 실험하기 시작했다. 수동적으로 작은 얼굴 이미지를 일탈적 3D 기하학 생성하는 두개골 사진으로 편집하고, 정점 변위의 대상 영역에 안면인식을 통해 기하학적 해체를 실행하는 방법을 실험하기 시작했다.

인류가 직면한 환경과 인공 지능에 관한 많은 문제는 분리되었다는 감정과 현실은 실제로 얽혀있음에도 불구하고 고립된 정체성에서 비롯된다고 느낀다. 기술이 우리를 죽음에서 구원해줄 수 있을까? 우리는 멸종할까? 그렇지 않다면 어떻게 될까? 아마도 이 작품은 이런 질문을 열어주는 데 도움이 될 수 있다.

나는 텍사스 중부 꽤 평범한 중형 도시에서 자랐고 항상 판타지보다는 공상과학에 더 매료되었었다. 십 대에는 오케스트라 튜바 연주자가 될 거라 생각했지만 음악 작곡과 사운드 디자인, 다음에는 악기 디자인, 더 최근에는 시청각 퍼포먼스와 갤러리 아트로 점차 옮겨갔다. 컴퓨테이션이 인류의 수행 능력 향상에 미칠 영향에 관심과 동시에 인류에 대한 혐오와 희망이 인류에 어떠한 영향을 줄 것인지에 관심이 있다.

기술은 미래 인류 생존에 역할을 해야 하지만 우리는 자연으로 돌아가 우리의 인프라에서 야생 생태계를 활용할 필요가 있다. 센서를 통해 자연을 알 수 있는 인류의 능력은 그 어느 때보다 강력하지만, 기술 자체는 매우 두꺼운 렌즈와 같이 우리를 가공의 것으로부터 격리하는 중개 구조적 역할을 한다. 대부분의 사람은 세계를 더 깊이 알기 위해 이를 사용하는 대신에, 기술의 중독적인 가상 현실에만 탐닉하고 있다.

기술은 인류에게 자연스럽다. 우리는 어떻게 공생의 정도를 향상시킬 수 있을까? 지구는 이미 생태계의 수명 주기에 제로-폐기물 지구 생명 지원 시스템을 개발했다. 더 나아가, 농업과 생태, 인간의 성장과 발전, 그리고 사이버 보안에 대해 깊이 연구하고 싶다.

I grew up in a fairly mundane, medium sized city in central Texas and was always more attracted to science fiction than fantasy. In my teens, I thought I would become an orchestral tuba player, but I gradually shifted to music composition and sound design, then instrument design, and more recently to audio-visual performance and gallery art. I am driven by the way that computation can synergize with and augment human performance and by a simultaneous misanthropy and hope for what humanity could become.

Technology must play a role in the future of human survival, but we also need to get back in touch with nature, and to leverage wild ecological processes in our infrastructure. Although humanity's capability to know nature through sensors is more powerful than ever before, technology itself is a very thick lens, an intermediary structure that insulates us from the non-man-made. Most people are not using it to know the world more deeply, instead becoming distracted by addictive stimulation.

Technology is natural to humanity. How do we improve our degree of symbiosis? The Earth has already developed a zero-waste global life support system in the life-cycles of ecosystems. Moving forward, I want to delve more deeply into agriculture and ecology, into human growth and development, and into cybersecurity.

ANATOLY RUDAKOV

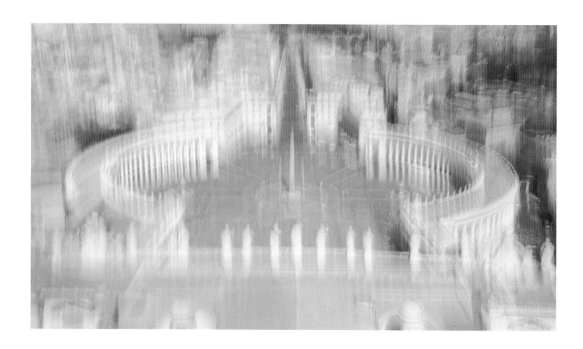

Anatoly Rudakov, *St. Petrus in Rome* (2016) (top), *Grand Palais* (2015) (bottom)

5 Cities of Anatoly Rudakov

by Barbara Rollmann-Borretty

Slowly, very slowly the names of five cities appear on the black screen of the monitor. And even slower thick and gleaming golden honey flows over the writing in a trickle. More and more of it covers the dark background, but then it becomes lighter and seems to glow. Gradually architectural shapes can be distinguished with in this mass of light and color. We can make out arches; an antique building ... the Roman Colosseum slowly appears in the dusk light.

This is the introduction to a 60 minutes video and it could not be more exiting. We are not allowed to dwell on the Colosseum for long, as in due course a trickle of liquid starts running down the screen again; soon it covers the whole width with its color. This time it is blue and cold, like glutinous water. The features of a face slowly appear and the contours of a head take shape. It is the head of a bronze statue belonging to the Roman emperor Augustus set up at the Via dei Fori Imperiali. The performance has begun.

Romeis the city we are looking at now, it is one ofthe five portrayed cities of this video collage. We are shown very personal impressions that Anatoly Rudakov has recorded in his pictures roaming the cities of London, Berlin, St. Petersburg, Paris and Rom. Being a photographer he is a genius in capturing the atmosphere of a cities architecture that only really comes to life through its magic mixture of light and movement.

Rudakovhas now composed a video from a selection of his photographs. He worked as a cameraman for three decades and in this video he has chosen to focus on the methodical work of film production. In this film moving pictures reach a state of art only through his camera work and his editing. The artist has a commanding knowledge of these tools. His video collage works with quickly changing contrasts, wide angel versus close-ups, hard versus soft, light versus dark. The direction of the video is done by the motives themselves with their enormous vitality. Compression or ambivalence, pausing and accelerating, even euphoria and dreariness, all these features of city are shown. None of the pictures remind of tourist attractions, even if monuments like the Colosseum, the Eiffel Tower or the Hermitage are shown.

The sequence in which the cities are presented

is distinctive but not in any way political; it is the pulse of everyday life. The rhythm of the changing pictures can not only be compared to the continuous flood of images we get swamped with daily through current affairs, but also of sudden changes that have an impact on us. While the author is watching this video in the artist's studio, the news comes in from Russia that a terrorist attack has taken place in the St. Petersburg underground. The present motive on the screen is covered with colored liquid as if it were the curtain of theatre stage and then it makes place for a completely new scene.

The style of the pictures is supposed to remind us of painting. The artist has an incredible gift of showing up structures that one doesn't easily see, just looking at an object briefly. These structures can be ornamental lines of squares and buildings, wavelike commotion in a crowd or simply the depth of a detail. This is part of the mystery, because every time we decode a motive, it is a new discovery for us. Parallel to this video another video sequence has been created that focuses on landscape. It is structured in the same method. Here the scenic aspects are of an even greater importance. The atmospheric pictures of all four seasons shine in amazing colors and show a great poetic and emotional potential.

Especially the very artistic transitions within both films have a close relation to painting. The overflow of pictures takes the part of the color that has to fill the canvas. Over and over again colorful pixel nets cover the displayed images and produce new pictures. Rudakov also likes to present his digital work like canvases in traditional wood frames.

The succession of the changing pictures has a strictly determined rhythm. It never lasts longer than one minute from the time one image shows up bit by bit on the screen until its complete appearance, it is then slowly infiltrated by a following one and then disappears completely. This rhythm reminds us of the turning of a film reel. The artist's description is brief: 60 Images in 60 Minutes. This is a guarantee for the dynamic of the film and also keeps it under control. Even though one could stop the video at any point, one of its main features is the time dimension. At one point the last picture fades away and the screen is blank again. Anatoly Rudakov's digital show is an incredibly aesthetic experience between photography, painting and film.

Anatoly Rudakov의 다섯 도시

Barbara Rollmann-Borretty

천천히, 매우 천천히 다섯 도시의 이름이 검은 모니터 화면에 보이기 시작했다. 그리고 더 느리고 두 껍고 매끈한 황금빛 꿀이 글 위로 흐른다. 점점 어두운 배경을 덮고, 그리고는 점점 밝아지며 빛이 난 다. 점차 건축적 형태는 빛과 색상으로 선명해진다. 아치 구조가 생긴다, 오래된 건물... 로마 콜로세움 은 천천히 황혼빛과 함께 나타난다.

이것이 60분짜리 비디오에 대한 흥미진진한 시작이다. 적당한 시기에 액체 물줄기가 다시 화면 아래 로 흐르기 시작하기에 우리는 콜로세움 이미지에 오랫동안 머물 수 없다. 곧 이 물줄기는 전체 폭을 덮고 이어서 차가운 푸른빛깔 끈적한 물이 흐른다. 얼굴의 특징이 천천히 나타나고 머리의 윤곽이 형 태를 띤다. 이는 "비아 데이 포리 임페리알리"에 세워진 로마 황제 아우구스투스의 청동 두상이다. 공 연은 시작되었다.

우리가 지금 보고 있는 도시인 Romeis는 이 비디오 콜라주의 다섯 개 도시 중 하나이다. 아나톨리 Rudakov가 런던, 베를린, 상트페테르부르크, 파리, 로마를 돌아다니며 기록한 사진에서 그의 매우 개 인적인 인상을 느낄 수 있다. 그는 빛과 움직임으로 살아 숨 쉬는 도시 건축물의 분위기를 포착하는 데 천재적이다.

Anatoly Rudakov, *Curly Trees* (2012) (top), *Oxford Street* (2014) (bottom)

Rudakov는 자신이 선택한 사진들로 비디오를 구성했다. 그는 30년간 카메라맨으로 일했으며 이 비디오에서 영화 제작의 체계적인 작업에 초점을 두어 작업했다. 이 영화에서 움직이는 그림은 그의 카메라 작업과 편집을 통해서 예술의 경지에 도달한다. 아티스트는 이러한 도구에 대한 전문적 지식을 갖추고 있다. 그의 비디오 콜라주는 빠르게 변화하는 넓은 시야각과 클로즈업, 단단함과 부드러움, 빛과 어둠 등의 대조를 다룬다. 그의 작품은 자료가 가지는 막대한 생동감을 바탕으로 제작된다. 응축성 혹은 양면성, 멈춤 혹은 가속, 심지어 행복감과 황량함까지 도시의 모든 모습을 보여준다. 콜로세움, 에펠탑, 또는 에르미타 쥬와 같은 기념물이 보이더라도 사진 중 관광 명소 같은 식상한 느낌은 들지 않는다.

도시를 보여주는 순서는 독특하지만 어떤 식으로든 정치적이지 않다. 이는 흔한 일상생활에 존재하는 방식이다. 변화하는 그림의 리듬은 우리가 일상생활에서 접하는 이미지의 홍수에 비유되기도 하며, 또는 우리에게 영향을 미치는 갑작스런 변화에도 비유될 수 있다. 필자가 스튜디오에서 이 작품을 보고 있는 동안 러시아 매체에서 상트페테르부르크 지하에서 테러공격이 발생했다는 속보가 흘러나온다. 화면에서 흘러내리는 형형색색의 액체들은 마치 새로운 장면을 위한 극장 무대의 커튼 같다.

이 사진들의 독특한 화풍은 회화 작품을 연상케 한다. 작가는 단순히 사물을 포착하는 것으로 우리가 쉽게 볼 수 없었던 구조를 강조하는 놀라운 재능을 가졌다. 이런 구조는 사각형과 건물의 미적인 선들이 될 수도, 군중의 흔들리는 소란 또는 단순한 깊이가 있는 섬세함 일수도 있다. 이는 수수께끼의 한 부분이다. 왜냐하 작가의 동기를 분석할 때마다 새로운 발견을 하기 때문이다. 이 비디오와 병행하여 풍경에 중점을 둔 다른 비디오 시퀀스가 만들어졌다. 이 둘은 같은 방법으로 구성됐다. 이기서는 풍경적 측면이 더욱 중요하다. 사계절의 분위기 있는 사진은 놀라운 색상으로 빛을 발하며 시적, 감성적 잠재력을 보여준다.

특히 두 영화의 예술적 전환은 회화와 밀접한 관계가 있다. 넘쳐흐르는 이미지들은 캔버스를 채우는 색상이 된다. 계속해서 다채로운 픽셀 그물이 기존의 이미지를 덮고 새로운 이미지를 만든다. Rudakov는 디지털 작품을 전통적인 회화를 위한 목재 프레임에 선보이기 선호한다.

변화하는 그림의 연속은 엄격히 정해진 리듬을 가지고 있다. 이미지가 한 이미지의 한 비트 한 비트씩 조금씩 나타나면 1분 이상 지속되지 않으며 다음 이미지에 천천히 침투 한 후 완전히 사라진다. 이러한 리듬은 필름 릴의 회전을 상기시킨다. 아티스트의 설명은 간단했다: "60 분에 60 이미지." 이것은 영화의 역동성을 보장이며 계속 제어하고 있다. 언제든지 비디오를 중단 할 수 있지만, 작품의 중요한 특징은 시간성에 있다. 작품에서 마지막 사진이 사라지고 화면이 다시 하얀 여백이 나온다. 아나톨리 Rudakov의 디지털 쇼는 사진, 그림 및 영화 사이의 놀라운 심미적인 경험이다.

Anatoly RUDAKOV (1951)는 유명한 러시아 다큐멘터리 사진 감독으로 그는 ZDF, ARTE, CBS, CNN, BBC, ARD, NHK, TBS 및 Discovery Channel www.ruan.tv와 협업했다. 모스크바 영화 학교 (VGIK)를 졸업하고 대학원생 때에는 소련 TV의 카메라맨으로 일하기도 했다. 최첨단의 정치, 경제 및 사회 문제에 관한 다큐멘터리를 촬영하면서 Anatoly는 러시아 북극의 아름다움, 중앙아시아, 동시베리아 툰드라 및 남부 러시아 대초원의 매혹적인 풍경을 포착했다. 2008 년 Anatoly는 모스크바를 떠나 독일 뮌헨으로 이주 후 현재 사진 작업에 집중하고 있다.

Anatoly Rudakov: Living Pictures - film translated in Photography Momentum Is Everything. Itchangesthevision, it sets in motion pictures and moving the viewer. The film,the "moving image" has found a technical counterpart for the dynamics of the world. Photographs Have a reputation of static: from flow of movements in the world, the camera takes a split second out, holding it, assures it, fixes it. Not so with Anatoly Rudakov. Rudakov Has Long Been a successful documentary film and television cameraman. This is not just seen in his picture at least, it's the core their photographic system. His images seem to move on before the viewer's face and escape the fixation. Here, the object is not lost, it does not disappear in the pure abstraction. Rather: The city lives, begins to vibrate, it generates patterns by hiding the unnecessary details from the viewer and focusing on the big shapes, color surfaces and the dynamics. With his new sense of "moving camera" Rudakov is close to the school of big movie camera men as Sergei Urusevskij, who has implemented brilliantly and masterly Mikhail Kalatosovs poetic visions of the real world (eg The cranes) in the 60s and 70s. Rudakov develops like Urusevskij his own visual language to express optimally, what he sees and wants the viewer to see. Rudakov has found an impressive way to translate photography into film.

Alexander Schwarz, PhD
(Film historian, Curator, Filmmaker – Tolle Idee Projekt agentur, Munich)

S/N

Aunt Johaha : A Taste of l'Avenir is an existential cooking blog and web presence test kitchen. The project is an exploration in flavor through the Tardis-like concept of 'the kitchen'. And it works through contemporary ideas of self expression through the development of a social media persona using a Dr. Who style framework of protagonistic-multiplicity.

The various Aunt Johahas of the ages express their feelings and impart wisdom through an interconnected aggregate of culinary joy on Tumblr. Each iteration of Aunt Johaha, favors slightly different culinary approaches and express themselves in a slightly different light and a different relationship to food.

Cooking blogs seek to share in an enthusiasm for flavor. Art blogs seek to contribute to the cultural context of the art world. Instagram showcases parts of our lives and careers and so on... By engaging in story building along with conceptual and culinary aggregation on multiple timelines and through a couple of formats (like a culinary blog) allows for a rambunctious and irreverent social commentary.

Relationships to food and culture, and relationships among women are explored and displayed in a familial context. Sharing pictures of the youngest Aunt Johaha (a meat loving giggling baby known as The Lion Shark) through the lens of contemporary art draws unexpected conclusions through its juxtaposition of content through the social media platform of Instagram. Using the language of food blogs to develop personas to comment on gender doubles back on itself in an ironic idiom.

S/N, *Lion Shark Johaha the IV states her desires* (top),
Lion Shark Johaha IV sings a hymn to sunshine for the bees (bottom)

S/N, Johaha II knows the secrets (top), *The taste of chocolate on the blade is like the magic of a unicorn : Johaha III* (bottom)

S/N, *Aunt Johaha II & III cross forks… Happenstance rings in the air* (top),
Dinner conversations between Johaha II & Guy Maddin (middle)
By *"Happenstance" Johaha II & III meet in the parallel universe (of Gary Hill)* (bottom)

Aunt Johaha : A Taste of l'Avenir 는 실존적인 요리 블로그이며 인터넷상에 존재하는 실험적 주방이다. 이 프로젝트는 Tardis와 같은 '주방'의 개념을 탐구한다. 블로그는 현대적 소셜미디어 페르소나를 통해 보여지는 자아 표현이라는 아이디어를 Dr. Who 스타일의 다중 주인공 체계를 이용한다 (Dr. Who: 1963년에 방송된 영국의 공상 과학 텔레비전 프로그램으로 주인공이 Tardis 라는 우주선을 타고 우주를 시간여행 하는 이야기를 다루고 있다). 다양한 연령대의 Aunt Johaha 들이 Tumblr에서 상호 연관되어 요리의 즐거움을 나누는 동시에 자신들의 감정을 표현하고 지혜를 전달한다. 개개의 반복되는 Aunt Johaha는 조금씩 다른 요리법을 추구하며 음식과 자신의 관계나 개인의 표현에도 차이를 띈다.

요리 블로그들은 맛에 대한 열정을 공유하는 데 심혈을 기울인다. 아트 블로그들은 예술세계에 문화적 문맥을 제공하기 위해 애쓴다. 인스타그램에서의 포스팅 진열은 우리의 삶이자 직업과 연관된 활동들이며 이는 끊임없이 이어진다. 다른 시간대에 다른 포맷으로 (예를 들어 요리 블로그) 개념적이면서도 요리의 집합적 요소에 이야기를 만드는 과정에 참여하는 작업은 난폭하면서도 때론 불손한 사회적 논평을 야기하기도 한다.

음식과 문화에 대한 관계나 여성들 간의 관계는 가족 간의 문맥에서 탐구되거나 표시되어 왔다. (고기 요리를 좋아하고 잘 키득거리는 The Lion Shark라고 불리는 아기인) 가장 어린 Aunt Johaha의 사진이 현대 예술의 렌즈를 통해 공유하는 과정은 소셜미디어 플랫폼인 인스타그램에서의 활동과 병치되며 예기치 않은 결말을 초래한다. 음식 블로그의 언어를 이용함으로써 페르소나를 발전시키는 과정은 성 역할에 논평을 남기며 역설적 관용구의 양면으로 비친다.

S/N is a multi-disciplinary art group, which works extensively with, but not limited to, video, sound, animation, photography, and mobile media. The exhibitions often include performative elements and mediated footage, pushing both experimental and conceptual ideas around media. S/N members include Jennida Chase and Hassan Pitts who have been collaborating since 2008, receiving grants and awards, and their work has been exhibited and screened world wide in various festivals, galleries and museums worldwide. Currently, Jennida serves as an Assistant Professor in the Department of Cinema and Photography and Hassan is the Technology Coordinator for the College of Mass Communication and Media Arts as well as the Executive Director of the Big Muddy Film Festival at Southern Illinois University Carbondale.

S/N은 다방면의 예술 분야에 활동하는 아티스트 그룹으로 구성된 그룹으로 비디오, 음향, 애니메이션, 사진, 그리고 모바일 미디어 등을 집중적으로 활용한다. 그들의 전시는 공연적 요소와 명상적 영상을 제시하며 미디어를 둘러싼 실험적이면서도 개념적인 아이디어를 연구한다. 다양한 수상 경력이 있는 S/N의 멤버인 Jennida Chase 와 Hassan Pitts 은 2008년부터 합동작업을 해 왔다. 그들의 작업은 세계의 여러 페스티벌과 갤러리 그리고 미술관을 통해 상영되거나 전시되었다. 현재 Jennida는 Southern Illinois University Carbondale에서 영상 사진학부의 조교수로 재직 중이며 Hassan 은 대중 매체와 미디어 아트의 기술 코디네이터 겸 Big Muddy Film Festival 의 수석 연출가로 활동하고 있다.

KAY YOON

1. Death and symbol

Death is a radical and inevitable phenomenon that all surface once dominated one's body is broken down into points. Line is a symbolic icon of essence that distinguishes life and death.

E RY H TH O L P E TO E S L
VE T I C L A S S O A I Y .

I would rather cry and do nothing than building a fragile object. But if I have to create a fragile object, I will shape the object, which is wrinkled, torn, and abandoned at all. I do not want to assign my weakness to other objects. Creation is a terrible and dangerous act. So I try to have self-consciousness in myself, but the finished work gains its own identity. It lives a separate history from the creator. It would be nice if the object does not blame me for making it fragile someday. I spent most of the phenomenon of being alive with the premise that I was born weak. Sometimes the creation itself seemed too violent and I have not found a place to run away.

Just one line cannot be violence. A number of lines gather to form a larger line. The formal and structural form takes away our nonlinear space everyday. We are educated not to be awakened and not to complain even if we were taken away of our curves and circles in daily life. Rather, sometimes we feel it is magnificent. For me, a concrete object does not mean

Kay Yoon, *Old Seoul* (top),
Old Seoul after War (bottom)

absolute grandeur. Repetition and grandeur of great size have always made me afraid. Like high-rise buildings, like Wagner's music .

Most visual artists believe they are taking advantage of this danger, but many of them misuse it. Magnificence is a mistake made only by the artist who wants to be a god. Creation is the easiest way to defend violence.

The object itself does not have the right force in it. So I hold an object. I attach functionality to an object. I give the object a name. Objects are still less attractive than text. I transcribe this result in a text form.

The moment I saw the bullet marks, I touched my death visually. When I was a child, I was sick and my dad took me to the ER, and I saw the face of devil. I could read his trace on the bullet marks. Countless death were taken over from this bullet marks on the wall, they are staring at me, as if they are jealous. I called my father. Dad! I hate death! Those who died from these bullets cannot dream of eternity, but the bullet marks that I copied can dream for eternity. How hilarious.

I put the gypsum on the wall. I see the face of death. I hear the whisper of the death dreaming of eternal life. I give the surface to the object. The gypsum particles which were only points become a fixed object with surfaces.

The boundary I used to know was mostly horizontal, and I came to Germany and experienced vertical boundaries. Korea: South and North, Germany: East and West. And finally I realized that there was neither vertical nor horizontal boundaries, but only the boundary itself. There is no change in the fact that there is a dichotomous. Men and women, sky and land, the energy of yin and yang that I were forced to learn as growing up in Asia have contributed a little more to making me a dichotomous person.

38383838383838383838383838383838383

welcome
to

38383838383838383838383838383838383

I feel lethargic before the threat of death.
I feel nonsense in front of the border.
I see death, its face.

Death likes the number 38. It is materialistic and tragic.
The boundary between living and dead exists in a nonlinear form.
Like a form of bullet marks, or like a form of a broken pottery, or any forms that you must have seen but not tried hard enough to remember.

2. Medium and death

The fantasy of development starts from the idea that the surfaces we artificially produced are the same as those of nature. The word "new" means fascination and threatening at the same time. We take it easy in the name of novelty before fear. Technically produced surfaces pretend and colonize the natural surfaces. We keep giving the surfaces where we are standing to technology. We have only lines left. So we feel threatened and turn into the digital world. In the digital space, there are countless numbers of points, numbered 0 and 1. In the digital world, we can not stand. We are trapped in this world.

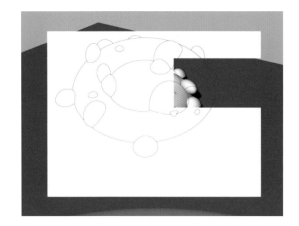

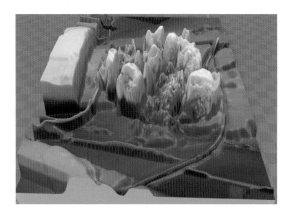

1. 죽음 그리고 상징

죽음은 몸을 지배하고 있던 표면이 점들로 해체되는 근본적이며 피할 수 없는 현상이다. 선은 삶과 죽음을 구별하는 본연에 대한 상징적 아이콘이다.

E R Y H T H O L P E T O E S L
V E T I C L A S S O A I Y .

허술한 것을 만들어낼 바에 차라리 나는 울어 버리고, 아무것도 하지 않을 것이다. 그러나 만약 허술한 무언가를 만들어야 한다면, 나는 아예 쭈글쭈글하고 찢어진, 그래서 결국은 버려지는 것을 만들겠다. 나는 나의 나약함을 다른 것에 반영시키고 싶지 않다. 창조란 끔찍하고 위험한 행위이다. 그래서 나는 스스로 그것을 의식하려고 하지만, 결국 완성된 작업은 그 스스로의 정체성을 갖게 된다. 그것은 창조자에서 떨어진 채 스스로의 역사를 살아간다. 나중에 그것이 허술하게 만든 것에 대해 나를 비난하지 않았으면 좋겠다. 나는 내가 약하게 태어났다는 전제 하에 살아있는 현상 대부분을 살았다. 때로는 창조 자체가 너무 폭력적으로 보이지만 나는 도망칠 곳을 찾지 못했다.

단 하나의 선은 폭력이 될 수 없다. 수많은 선이 모여 하나의 커다란 선의 형태가 된다. 형식적이고 구조적인 형태는 매일 우리의 비선형적인 공간을 빼앗는다. 우리는 일상에서 곡선과 원을 빼앗겼다 하더라도 깨달음을 얻거나 불평을 하지 말라고 교육받았다. 오히려 우리는 그것이 훌륭하다고 느낀다. 나에게 구체적 대상은 절대적인 장엄함을 의미하지 않는다. 반복과 커다란 규모의 장엄함은 언제나 나를 두렵게 만든다. 바그너의 음악이나 같은 고층 건물처럼 말이다.

대부분의 시각 예술가들은 그들이 이 위험을 이용한다고 믿고 있지만, 그들 대부분은 이것을 잘못 사용하고 있다. 장엄함이란 신이 되고 싶은 예술가가 만들어낸 하나의 실수이다. 창조란 폭력을 방어하는 가장 쉬운 방법이다.

사물 그 자체는 알맞은 힘을 갖고 있지 않다. 나는 사물에 기능을 부여한다. 나는 사물에게 이름을 부여한다. 사물은 여전히 텍스트보다 덜 매력적이다. 나는 이 결과를 텍스트의 형태로 기록한다.

이 총알 자국들을 보는 순간, 나는 나의 죽음을 시각적으로 느낀다. 내가 어렸을 때 아파서 나의 아버지가 나를 응급실로 데려간 적이 있다. 나는 거기서 악마의 얼굴을 보았다. 나는 총알 자국들 위에서 그의 흔적을 알아챌 수 있었다. 수많은 죽음들이 벽 위의 총알 자국으로부터 넘어왔다. 그것들은 나에게서 시작되었으며, 그들은 마치 질투하듯이 나를 응시하고 있었다. 나는 나의 아버지를 불렀다. 아빠! 나는 죽음이 싫어요! 이 총알로써 죽은 이들은 영원을 꿈꿀 수 없지만, 내가 복제한 총알 자국은 영원을 꿈꿀 수 있다. 얼마나 우스꽝스러운가.

나는 벽 위의 석고를 바른다. 나는 죽음의 얼굴을 본다. 나는 영원한 삶을 꿈꾸는 죽음의 속삭임을 듣는다. 나는 사물에게 표면을 선사한다. 오직 점들이었던 석고 입자들이 표면 위에서 고정된 사물이 된다.

내가 알고 있던 경계는 대부분 수평적이었다. 그리고 독일에 와서 나는 수직적인 경계들을 경험하게 되었다. 한국은 남과 북으로 구분되고, 독일은 동과 서로 구분된다. 나는 결국 수직적 경계도, 수평적 경계도 없으며, 단지 경계 자체만이 있음을 깨달았다. 이분법이 존재한다는 사실에는 변함이 없다. 남성과 여성, 하늘과 땅, 음양의 에너지와 같이 내가 아시아에서 배워야 했던 것들은 나를 더욱 이분법적 인간으로 만들었다.

3838383838383838383838383838383838383838383838
welcome
to
3838383838383838383838383838383838383838383838

죽음의 위협 전에 나는 무기력함을 느낀다.

경계 앞에서 나는 의미 없음을 느낀다.

나는 죽음을, 이것의 얼굴을 본다.

죽음은 38이라는 숫자를 좋아한다. 이 숫자는 물질주의적이고 비극적이다.

살아있는 것과 죽은 것의 경계는 비직선 형태 안에 존재한다.

총알 자국의 형태, 또는 부서진 도자기의 형태, 또는 당신이 기억하려고 노력하지는 않았지만 분명히 당신이 본 적 있는 어떤 형태 말이다.

2. 매체와 죽음

개발에 대한 환상은 우리가 인공적으로 만들어낸 모습들이 자연의 모습들과 동일하다는 생각에서 출발한다. '새로움'이라는 단어는 매혹적이기도 하지만 동시에 위협적이다. 우리는 두려움 이전에 참신함이라는 이름을 쉽게 받아들인다. 기술적으로 생산된 모습들은 자연적인 모습인 체하며, 또 그것에 대량 서식한다. 우리는 기술을 고집하는 곳에 계속 표면을 부여한다. 우리에게는 오직 선들만이 남아있다. 그래서 우리는 위협을 느끼고 디지털 세계로 돌아섰다. 디지털 공간에는 0과 1로 매겨진 수많은 점들이 있다. 디지털 세계에서 우리는 설 수 없다. 우리는 이 세계에 갇혀있다.

Kay Yoon is a new media artist based in Seoul, Korea and Nuremberg, Germany. She is currently studying at the Academy of fine Art in Nuremberg, Germany. By drawing the metamorphosis of nonliving organisms and digitizing them, the artist tried to reposition the digital materiality in art.
Nuremberg, where the artist lives, is considered to be among the most bombed cities in Germany during World War II. It shows how a culture has undergone a change in history. She has made her works by imprinting the remaining bullet marks in the cities with a plaster model and reconstructing it with a 3D program, and printing them with various sizes and colors.

Kay Yoon은 독일 서울과 뉘른베르크에서 활동하는 뉴 미디어 아티스트이다. 그녀는 현재 독일 뉘른베르크 (Nuremberg)의 미술 아카데미 (Academy of Fine Art)에서 공부하고 있다. 무생물 유기체의 변형을 그리고 디지털화함을 통해 작가는 디지털 물질성에 대해 의문을 던진다.
작가가 살고있는 뉘른베르크 (Nuremberg)는 2차 대전 중 독일에서 가장 피해를 입은 지역이다. 이 도시의 문화는 역사의 격변을 그대로 담아내고 있다. 그녀는 도시에 남아있는 총알 자국을 석고로 캐스팅 후 컴퓨터 3D 프로그램으로 재구성하고, 다양한 색상과 크기로 출력하는 작업을 하였다.

JUSTYNA ADAMCZYK

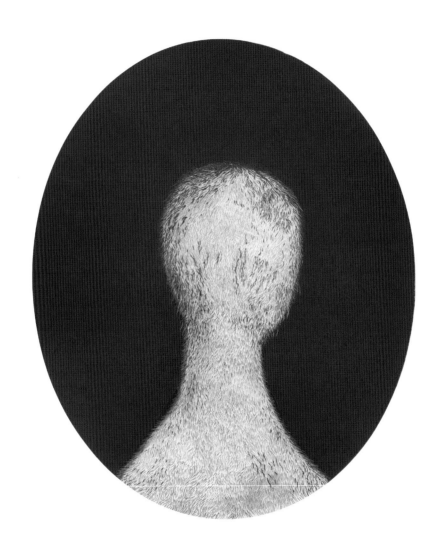

Justyna Adamczyk, *Fur* (2016)

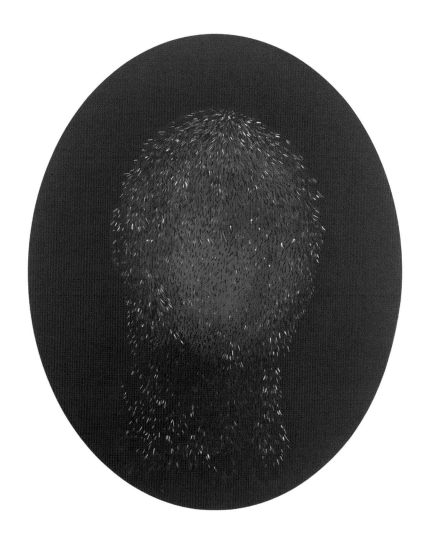

Justyna Adamczyk, *Bold* (2016)

Justyna Adamczyk, *Rotten* (2016)

Justyna Adamczyk (b. 1981 Opoczno) Rceived MFA from the E. Gepperd's Academy of Fine Arts in Poland, Wroclaw, painting specialization in 2007. She received an award of Ministry of Culture and Heritage (twice, in 2005 and 2006). Since 2005 she participates in many exhibitions and contests in Poland and abroad. Her works were exhibited on Pyeongchang Biennale & Gangneung Folk Art Festival 2017(Gangneung South Korea), Foksal Gallery Fundation (Warsaw), Vienna Art Fair (Vienna) , or on Heppen Transfer Gallery (Warsaw), Gryffin Gallery (London) Berlin Blue Art Space (Berlin) Best regards Galery (Frankfurt), EC Gallery (Chicago), BWA (Bielsko Biała and Wroclaw) or Steps Gallery, PolArt Fertival (Melbourne) Her works were distinguished as part of contests such as: Biennale, Bielska Jesień (2013,Public Galery, Bielsko Biała), 9th Geppert's Contest (2009, BWA Awangarda Wrocław), Biennale „Bielska Jesień" (2009, Public Gallery, Bielsko Biała), „Promocje" 17th Young Artists Contest (2007 Legnica). She lives and works in Warsaw, Poland.

Justyna Adamczyk (1981년 폴란드 Opoczno 태생)는 2007년 폴란드 브로프와츠의 E. Gepperd's Academy of Fine Arts에서 회화 전공 석사를 마쳤다. Justyna는 2005년과 2006년, 두 번에 걸쳐 Ministry of Culture and Heritage 상을 받았다. 2005년부터 Justyna는 폴라드를 포함한 세계 각국에서 수많은 전시와 대회에 참여했다. 그녀의 작업은 2017년 한국의 평창 비엔날레와 가평 포크 아트 페스티벌에서 전시되었고, 바르샤바의 Foksal 갤러리 파우데이션, 비엔나의 비엔나 아트페어, 바르샤바의 Heppen Transfer 갤러리, 런던의 Gryffin 갤러리, 베를린의 블루 아트 스페이스, 프랑크푸르트의 Best regards 갤러리, 시카고의 EC 갤러리, 비엘스코비아와 바르샤바의 BWA, Steps 갤러리, 멜버른의 PolArt 페스티벌에서 소개되었다. 또한 Justyna의 작품은 Bielska Jesień 비엔날레 (2013,Public 갤러리, 비엘스코비아), 제 9회 Geppert's 콘테스트 (2009, BWA Awangarda Wrocław), Bielska Jesień 비엔날레 (2009, Public 갤러리, 비엘스코비아), "Promocje" 제17회 청년 작가 콘테스트 (2007 레그니차) 등의 대회에서 두각을 나타냈다. 그녀는 현재 폴란드의 바르샤바에서 활동하고 있다.

MARYAMSADAT AMIRVAGHEFI

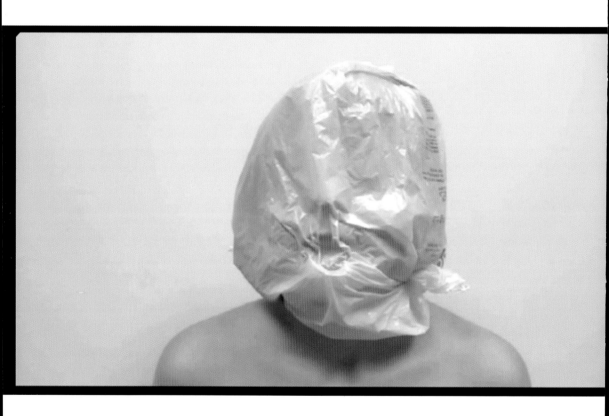

Maryam sadat Amirvaghefi, *Keep Your Heads Up and Shut Up* (2016), still images from Digital Video

INJURED DURING WARM UP

by Maryamsadat Amirvaghefi

I was warming up
I had been waiting four years for these games
It was important to me
Everyone knew I was the best Iranian Gymnast
My body was completely covered
I wanted to return to Iran after that game
It was too tight; they could see all of my bones
I covered my body with a big flag until the final moment
I heard my name announced from the speakers
MARYAMSADAT AMIRVAGHEFI, from Iran
I arrived at the floor
I somersaulted
There was no applause
Everyone seemed shocked with my perfect form
I was running and jumping
I looked like a butterfly
Everyone started to cheer for me
They showered me with flowers
Without a doubt, I deserved the gold medal
When my feet touched the ground, I bowed
The cheering voices disappeared slowly
For about 5 minutes, it was pitch black
Suddenly they turned on the lights
They called my name again
I was shocked
I kept performing when the lights went out
Did anyone see my performance?

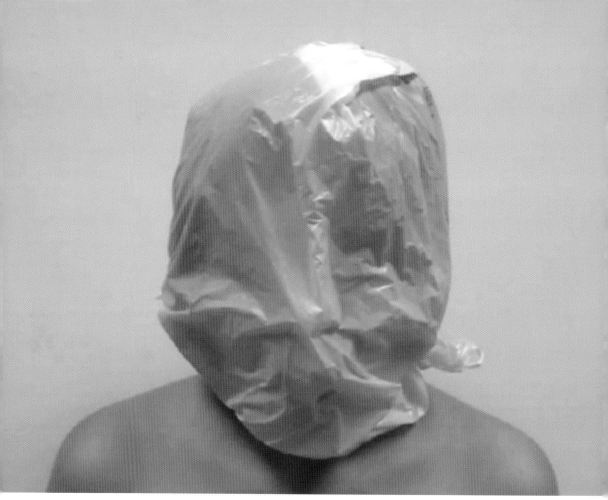

Maryam sadat Amirvaghefi, *Keep Your Heads Up and Shut Up* (2016), still from Digital Video

"Who won the game? Who won the game?"

It is just competition. It's difficult for me to talk about being a winner or loser, as I've never experienced either completely. When an individual faces a situation where they feels here is no chance to succeed, it often result in a sense of pity. At that point, an individual has a decision: accept the situation and pity yourself: or to become a fighter that doesn't look over your shoulder and push forward trying to prove the naysayers wrong.

I have put myself at the center of the work. By focusing on the autobiographical, I am able to evaluate different points of view that align with political issues, nationalities, and my personal life. My trip to Iran last summer that took three months effect on my work a lot. When I came back here, I saw myself as a person who feels uncertain about everything. According to the social and political issues I cannot belong myself to either of these two countries. In addition, when I look at myself I see a woman, who is from Middle East and living in a USA, which is complicated enough for making work about.

 I have found myself asking the following question: if I were to win, does the game end and will I have incentive to continue?

준비운동 중의 부상

나는 가볍게 준비하고 있었다.
4년 후 나는 올림픽 경기에 출전했다 나에겐 중요한 일이었다
모든 사람들이 나를 최고의 이란 선수로 알고 있다
내 몸은 완전히 덮였다
난 경기 후 이란으로 돌아가고 싶었다
옷이 너무 꽉 껴서 사람들은 내 골격을 훤히 볼 수 있을 것이다
마지막 순간까지 커다란 국기로 내 몸을 싸맸다
스피커를 통해 내 이름이 호명되었다
MARYAMSADAT ASMIRVAGHEFI, 이란
바닥으로 갔다
내 몸은 붕 떴다
아무도 손뼉 치지 않았다
나는 사람들이 내 완벽함에 놀란 것이라 생각했다
나는 달렸고, 뛰었고, 나는 훌륭했다, 나비처럼 보였다
모두가 날 응원하기 시작했다, 꽃을 던졌고, 계속 던지고 던지고
던졌다.
난 금메달을 받기에 여지가 없었다.
내 발이 땅에 닿을 때, 난 인사했다
응원의 목소리가 천천히 사라졌다
한 5분간 모든 것이 깜깜했다
갑자기 불이 켜졌고
내 이름을 다시 호명했다!
난 충격을 받았다!
내 차례 때 불이 꺼졌다고
누구도 내 공연을 보지 못했다...

"누가 이겼어? 누가 이겼어?"

이건 그냥 경기일 뿐이다. 난 완전한 승자나 패자로서의 경험이
없기 때문에, 그런 것들에 대해 말하는 것은 어려운 일이다. 한 개
인이 어떠한 상황에서 성공할 기회가 없다는 사실에 직면할 때
그 끝에 느끼는 감정은 대부분 연민이다. 그 순간, 그는 결정하게
된다: 상황을 받아 들이고 자신을 스스로 가엾이 여기거나 : 또는
반대하는 사람들이 틀렸다는 것을 증명하기 위해 미리 걱정하지
말고 앞으로 나아가 싸우는 것.

나는 무언가에 굉장히 집중했던 적이 있다. 나는 자서전을 만들면
서, 다른 시점에서의 정치적 이슈, 국적 그리고 나의 인생을 나란
히 하고 평가할 수 있었다. 지난여름, 3개월 동안 갔었던 이란 여
행은 내 작업에 많은 영향을 끼쳤다. 내가 이곳에 돌아왔을 때,
나는 모든 것에 대해서 확신할 수 없어 하는 나 자신을 볼 수 있
었다. 사회, 정치적 이슈에 있어 나 스스로 두 나라 어디에도 속할
수 없었다. 또한 중동 출신의 미국에 사는 여성이라는 나의 정체
성에 관한 작업을 하기란 굉장히 어려운 과제다

스스로 다음과 같은 질문을 던졌다:
만약 내가 이겼었더라면, 게임이 끝나고 나는 계속할 수 있는 해
택을 받았을까?

Maryam sadat Amirvaghefi was born in Tehran, Iran in 1989. Amiravghefi studio practice encompases mixed media paintings, videos, and sculpture pieces. Amirvaghefi is a MFA candidate at the University of Arkansas, Fayetteville, and holds a BFA from Sooreh University in Tehran. Amiravghefi has been included in group shows in Tehran and USA and her works have been published in Studio Visit Magazine and Average Art Magazine. As a curator, she recently organized "Running Towards Dreams", an exhibition shown in Iran and the US, which featured twenty one emerging artists from both countries. She lives and works in Fayetteville, Arkansas.

Maryam sadat Amirvaghefi는 이란의 수
도 테헤란에서 1989년에 태어났다. Amirvaghefi 스튜디오 연습은 혼합 매체 페인
팅, 비디오 및 조각 작품을 했다. Amir-
vaghefi는 페이트빌에 위치한 아칸소 대
학교에서 석사 졸업 예정이고, 테헤란의
Sooreh University에서 학사 학위를 받았
다. Amiravghefi는 테헤란과 미국에서 진
행된 그룹 전시에 참여한 경험이 있고, 그
녀의 작품은 Studio Visit 잡지와 Average
Art 잡지를 통해 출판되었다. 큐레이터로서
그녀는 최근 이란과 미국에서 전시된 스물
한 명의 떠오르는 예술가들을 발굴하기 위
한 "Running Towards Dreams"를 기획했
다. 그녀는 미국 아칸소주의 페이트빌에서
거주하며 작업을 하고 있다.

The idea behind Rami came during a study about beats phenomenon: an acoustic interference, produced by two or more sine waves with slightly different frequency, which results in a periodic amplitude modulation. Looking at a naked tree I imagined it as a score where a set of frequency moving near and away, crossing each others, following the branch's shape and creating complex beats patterns. In Rami the sound is created by a sonifcation process of shape and movements of the tree showed in the video component.

그의 아이디어는 Rami 라는 프로그램과 맥노리 현상 (비트 페노미넌) 연구 중 발전되었다. 맥노리 현상은 진폭 변조 주기들의 결과물로 도출된 미묘한 차이를 가진 주파수와 두 개 혹은 그 이상의 사인 웨이브에서 도출된 음향 장애로부터 발생한다. 헐벗은 나무들을 보면서 그것이 근경 혹은 원경에서 움직이는 주파수들의 세트라고 상상했다. 나뭇가지들의 형태를 따라 서로를 가로지르며 복잡한 비트 패턴을 만들어낸다. Rami에서 나무의 형태와 움직임은 소리로 변환된다.

Alfredo Ardia, Rami (2015), stills from Digital Video

Born in 1989 in South Italy, Alfredo Ardia was fascinated by sound, its perception and how it relates with other media, exploring sound phenomena of elementary sound entities and its behaviors. In his audiovisual works, characterized by a gentle synergy between the two components, he uses visual elements as a sound score through sonification processes, and sound visualization tools as visual elements, creating an entity which can be perceived both through hearing and sight. Lovers of a calm life, he is inspired by nature and daily surrounding contexts.

1989년 이탈리아 남부에서 태어난 Alfredo Ardia는 음향과 그에 대한 인식, 그리고 음향이 다른 미디어와 연관되는 방식에 매료되었다. 그의 시청각 작업은 두 요소 (시각과 청각) 사이의 섬세한 시너지 효과로 특징지을 수 있다. 그는 소니피케이션 (초음파파쇄) 과정을 통해 얻은 사운드 스코어들과 사운드 시각 장치들을 시각적 요소로 이용한다. 그의 작업들은 시각과 청각, 양쪽 모두에서 인지 가능한 개체들로 탄생한다. Alfredo Ardia는 평화로운 삶의 연인들, 즉 자연과 일상 속 주변 환경들로부터 영감을 얻는다.

Alfredo Ardia, *Rami* (2015), stills from Digital Video

WHITNEY BANDEL

My artwork investigates the relationships between controversial technologies, media, and user interactivity. Through my research I aim to personalize politics, give them a physical platform, and provide a middle ground to foster social consciousness and communication. By encouraging my audience to actively engage with social and political issues through interactive media, it is my goal to spread social awareness. The intention of my work is not to influence or orchestrate a desired social or political opinion, but to build a platform where participants can openly communicate verbally and physically with one another. Participants are encouraged to interact with the artwork and each other through controllers and gestures, allowing them to actively engage in various roles within a simulated environment that acts as a microcosm of contemporary sociopolitical issues. These interactions and performances are then documented as a reflection on our present culture.

Shoot 'em Up! is an interactive video piece. The interactive components for the piece consist of headphones, buttons, and controllers that users can interact with. To operate the video, users must place the headphones over their ears and interact with the controls. On the button console there are two buttons, one switches out targets that can be fired at, the other switches out firearms. The former changes the person and location in which you can fire at, the latter changes out the audio effect that you can hear when the shots are fired. In order to shoot, the user must pick up one of the two pistol shaped controllers, aim the barrel at their mouths, and speak into it. This triggers a microphone sensor that registers the volume as a shot, which then triggers a video effect visualizing the shooting.

When the shooters speak out their aggressions towards these targets, they are forced to simultaneously direct these negative gestures at themselves. By speaking their aggressions instead of pressing a button mindlessly, they are made to feel cognizant of their actions and take ownership of them. This piece is designed not only for those who actively engage with the controls, but also spectators who can watch from other areas of the gallery as they witness these interactions.

Whitney Bandel, *RGB Depth Test with Kinect* (2015), Self portrait

나의 작품은 논란의 여지가 있는 기술과 미디어, 사용자 상호 작용을 다룬다. 이 연구를 통해 정치를 개인화하고 물리적인 플랫폼을 제공하며 사회 인식과 의사소통을 촉진하기 위한 중개적 역할을 하고자 한다. 인터렉티브 매체를 통해 관람객들이 사회 및 정치 문제에 적극적으로 참여하도록 장려함으로써 사회 인식을 확산시키는 것이 본인의 목표다. 내 작품의 의도는 개인의 사회적 또는 정치적 의견에 영향을 미치거나 조율하는 것이 아니라 참여자들이 서로 언어나 신체로 편하게 의사소통할 수 있는 플랫폼을 구축하는 것이다. 참여자들은 컨트롤러와 동작을 통해 작품과 참여자들끼리 상호 작용하도록 장려되고, 현대 사회에서의 정치적 문제의 축소판인 시뮬레이션 환경에서 다양한 역할을 적극적으로 수행할 수 있다. 이런 상호 작용과 수행 방식은 현재의 문화에 대한 반영으로 기록된다.

Shoot 'em Up! 은 인터렉티브 영상 작업이다. 이 작품의 인터렉티브 구성 요소는 사용자가 상호 작용할 수 있는 헤드폰, 버튼 및 컨트롤러로 구성된다. 영상을 작동시키기 위해서 사용자는 헤드폰을 끼고 컨트롤을 조작해야 한다. 버튼 콘솔에는 두 개의 버튼이 있다. 하나는 발포할 타깃을 선택할 수 있고, 다른 하나로는 총기를 바꾼다. 첫 번째 버튼은 발사할 수 있는 사람과 위치를 변경하며, 두 번째 버튼은 발시 나오는 오디오 효과를 변경한다. 발포하려면 사용자는 반드시 두 개의 권총 모양의 컨트롤러 중 하나를 잡고 자신의 입안에 총구를 겨눈 상태로 말해야 한다. 음량을 발포로 등록해 놓은 마이크로폰 센서가 방아쇠가 되어 '총쏘기'를 시각화한 비디오 효과를 상영한다.

발포자가 타깃을 향해 적의를 토하면 그들은 부정적인 제스처를 동시에 자신에게 향하게 된다. 무의식중에 버튼을 누르는 대신 그들의 적의를 말함으로 그들은 자신들이 행동을 인식하면서 의식하게 된다. 이 작품은 적극적으로 참여하는 사람들뿐 아니라 전시장 내에서 바라보고 있는 관중들도 이런 상호 작용을 목격할 수 있도록 설계되었다.

Whitney Bandel, *Shoot 'em Up! installation documentation,* stills from installation

Whitney Bandel, *Shoot 'em Up! installation documentation*, still from installation

Whitney Bandel is a new media artist and educator. She began her studies in traditional media, exploring drawing, painting, and fibers. From there she went on to explore digital media through her MFA in Time Arts at Northern Illinois University. Her thesis research explored the relationships between controversial technologies, media, and user interactivity. Currently her artwork explores sociopolitical topics on media and technology utilizing user interaction through controllers and gestures. She teaches at Kansas State University and Johnson County Community College in Kansas, USA. Recent select exhibitions include: Social and Politically Engaged Art, 4th annual multi-national 2016 FL3TCH3R Exhibit, Reece Museum, East Tennessee State University, TN; iDEAS Exhibition, International Digital Media and Arts Association Conference 2016, Winona State University, MN; and Tactile, Visual Art Exchange, NC.

Whitney Bandel은 뉴 미디어 아티스트이자 교육자이다. 드로잉, 회화 및 섬유와 같은 전통 매체 연구로부터 시작하여, Northern Illinois University에서 Time Arts 전공으로 대학원을 다니며 디지털 미디어로 영역을 확장하였다. 그녀의 논문은 논란이 되고 있는 기술, 미디어, 사용자 상호 작용에 관해 다루었다. 현재 그녀의 작업은 컨트롤러와 동작을 이용해 사용자 상호 작용을 유도하는 기술과 미디어에 대한 사회 정치적 이슈들을 다룬다. 그녀는 미국 캔자스에 있는 Kansas State University와 Johnson county Community College에서 학생을 가르치고 있다. 최근 Social and Politically Engaged Art와 제4회 국제전 2016 FL3TCH3R, Reece 미술관, 동 테네시 주립대학; iDEAS 전, 2016 국제 디지털 미디어와 아트 협회 콘퍼런스, 위노아 주립대학, MN; and Tactile, Visual Art Exchange, NC 등에 참여하며 활발히 활동하고 있다.

D S CHAPMAN

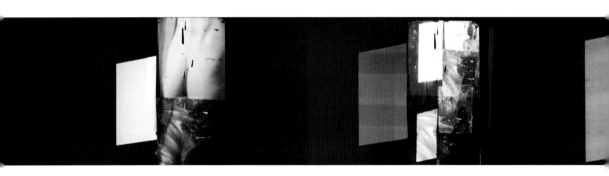

Mirrors are central to our self-perception, as is noted by the psychoanalyst Jacques Lacan in his influential essay, "Mirror Stage." The mirror allows us to not only see ourselves, but to recognize ourselves. This is something that can be difficult for transgender people, especially those struggling with gender dysphoria. The act of looking into the mirror becomes an act of looking through oneself to see one's true self. Rather than revealing something, the mirrored image is an obstruction. Mirror gazing is typically related to narcissism, though this assumes that the looker is admiring what is visible: often trans people are looking for something that they cannot see in their reflections.

Narcissism is something that Rosalind Krauss dissects in "Video: The Aesthetics of Narcissism." With the introduction of readily available video technology, a new kind of art was introduced into the contemporary art scene. The body was material and the self was the subject, with video acting as a mirror that doubles as a record. This was, and still is extremely important for minority groups, especially trans people, who have to create representation for themselves. Through the construction of a closed-circuit system, I created a narcissistic dialogue with a mirror, producing a looping video portrait that visualizes the fragmentation and layering of my identity.

거울은 정신분석사 자크 라캉의 유명한 에세이 "Mirror Stage"에서 지적한 것처럼 자기 인식의 핵심이다. 거울은 우리 자신을 볼 뿐만 아니라 자신을 인식할 수 있게 해준다. 이는 트렌스젠더, 특히 성 정체성 장애로 어려움을 겪고 있는 사람들에게는 어려운 일일 수 있다. 거울을 들여다보는 행위는 진짜 자기 자신을 보면 들여다보는 행위가 된다. 반사된 이미지는 무언가를 드러내기보다는 방해물이 된다. 거울을 지그시 바라보는 것은 전형적으로는 자기애와 관련이 있다는 말은 거울을 보는 이유가 그들이 눈에 보이는 것을 동경한다는 전제하에 성립한다. 트렌스젠더들은 반사된 그들의 모습이 아닌, 눈으로 볼 수 없는 무언가를 마주치길 원한다.

로잘린 크라우스 Rosalind Krauss는 "비디오: 나르시시즘의 미학 Video: The Aesthetics of Narcissism"에서 나르시시즘을 상세히 분석했다. 쉽게 사용할 수 있는 비디오 기술의 도입과 함께 새로운 종류의 예술이 현대 미술계에 소개되었다. 몸은 재료이고 자아는 주제이며 카메라는 거울과도 같이 이를 복제한다. 이는 소수, 특히 자신의 표상을 만들어야만 하는 트렌스 피플 들에게는 매우 중요한 문제다. 난 폐쇄된 순환 시스템 구축을 통해 내 정체성이 균열되고 허물에 쌓인 것을 시각적으로 볼 수 있게 거울과 나르시시트적 대화를 하는 나의 모습을 반복 재생 영상 초상화로 만들었다.

D S Chapman, *Never met a mirror (s)he didn't like* , stills from digital video

D S Chapman, *Never met a mirror (s)he didn't like* , still from digital video

D S Chapman is a Texas-born artist, organizer, and cultural producer based in San Diego, who is invested in the contemporary representation of trans people in art and culture. Working across media and performance, the artist explores the construction of gender as a foundation for identity, relationships, and ritual. They are a founding member of DADE, a burgeoning feminist collective dedicated to providing a platform for women and femme artists. Chapman's work has been exhibited and screened internationally in museums and artist-run spaces including the Czong Institute of Contemporary Art, RAIZVANGUARDA Associacao Cultural, and Altes Finanzamt.

D S Chapman은 텍사스 출신의 예술가이자 조직자이며 샌디에이고에 기반을 둔 문화 프로듀서로, 예술과 문화의 트랜스 피플의 현대적 표상을 만드는 데 힘쓰고 있다. 미디어와 퍼포먼스 전반에 걸쳐 작업하면서 작가는 정체성, 관계 및 의식의 기초로서 남녀 정체성 형성을 탐구한다. 그들은 여성과 여성 예술가를 위한 플랫폼을 제공하기 위해 전념하는 급증하고 있는 여성주의자 모임 DADE의 창립 멤버이다. Chapman의 작품은 국제적으로 CICA미술관을 포함, RAIZVANGUARDA Associacao Cultural, Altes Finanzamt 등의 미술관과 예술가-운영 공간에서 전시 및 상영되었다.

JESSICA DOLENCE

Jessica Dolence, *Virtual Bizarre Silk*

Jessica Dolence, *The Blue Room (2016),* still from installation

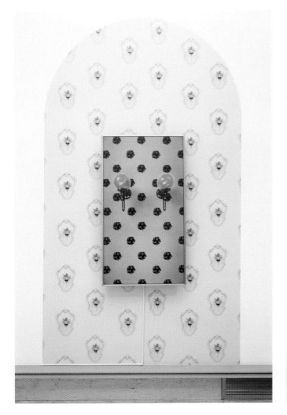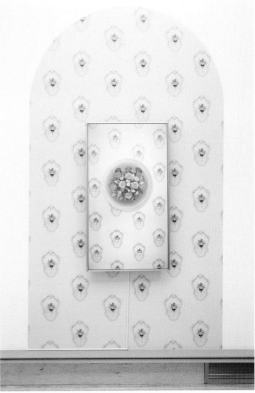

Jessica Dolence, *A View with a Room* (2016), stills from installation

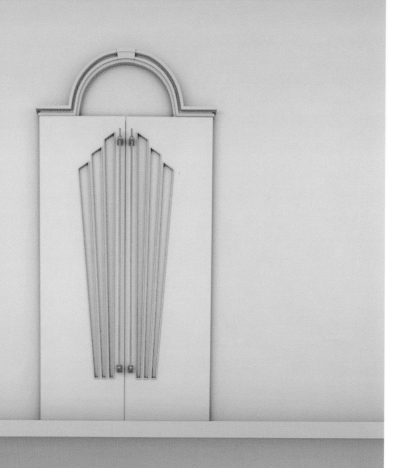

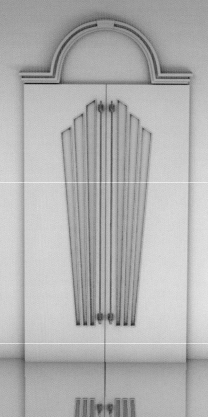

Jessica Dolence, *A View with a Room, Elevator Scene* (2016), still from digital video

I'm interested in digital decoration and ornamentation in relationship to CyberFeminism and virtual interior design. I design animated wallpaper that is ambient, and subversive. The wall, screen, and monitor are all habitats for my work. When projected and mapped onto a wall, the wallpaper alters space and the background becomes the subject. I'm influenced by 20th Century historic cultural trends, period film sets, and Internet sub genres like Sea Punk. Coloration and pattern design are used to talk about the spectrum of femininity.

I use 3D modeling software and After Effects to build sets and decorative architectural models to build imagery. A 3D environment, once built, provides the ability to rapidly modify materials and lifts the restrictions of reality. Time based media allows my work to live and breath. My newest body of work will continue to cross-pollinate material and concept, using projection mapping, surface design and 3D printed objects to further blur relationships between art and technology.

BFA in Intermedia at The Herberger Institute of Design and the Arts at Arizona State University. Prior to graduate school at Jessica was a member of SOIL Gallery, an artist run space, and is a freelance visual designer. In July 2015 The Blue Room exhibited at Interstitial Gallery in Seattle. In May 2016 EO1 Electric Objects released a commissioned collection of narrative video works titled A View With a Room, and Edith's Garden in November. She has also exhibited with Cybertwee Headquarters, a VR group installation.

사이버 페미니즘과 가상 인테리어 디자인상에 있어 기상 공간 디자인이 어떠한 역할을 하는지에 관심이 있다. 난 은은하면서도 파괴적인 애니메이션 벽지를 디자인한다. 벽과 스크린, 모니터 모두 내 작업 환경이다. 프로젝터가 벽을 비추거나 매핑할 때 벽지는 공간을 바꾸고 배경은 주제가 된다. 내 작업은 20세기 역사적 문화트렌드, 시대 영화 세트, Sea Punk와 같은 인터넷 하위 장르의 영향을 받았다. 색상과 패턴 디자인은 여성성의 스펙트럼에 대해 이야기하는 데 사용됐다.

3D 모델링 소프트웨어와 After Effects를 사용해 세트 및 장식용 건축 모델을 제작해서 이미지를 만든다. 한 번 구축된 3D 환경은 재료를 빠르게 수정하고 현실의 한계를 뛰어넘을 수 있다. 시간성이 있는 매체는 내 작업을 살아 숨 쉬게 한다. 최근의 작업에서는 프로젝션 매핑과 표면 디자인 및 3D 프린터를 이용해 물질과 개념을 지속적으로 융합하고 이를 통해 예술과 기술의 경계를 허물고자 한다.

Jessica Dolence는 시애틀을 기점으로 하는 예술가이자 디자이너이다. 그녀는 Cranborrok Academy of Art에서 MFA를 The Herberger Institute of Design and the Arts at Arizona State University에서 Intermedia로 BFA를 받았다. 졸업하기 전 Jessica는 아티스트 런 스페이스인 SOIL 갤러리의 멤버였고 프리랜서 비주얼 디자이너였다. 2015년 7월 The Blue Room이 시애틀에 있는 Interstitial Gallery에 전시되었다. 2016년 5월 EO1 Electric Objects는 A View With Room이라는 제목의 서사 비디오 작품을, 11월에는 Edith's Garden의 컬렉션을 발표했다. 그녀는 Cybertwee Headquaters와 함께 가상현실 설치 전시를 진행했다.

BEN EHRMANN

By Joy Miller

Unglamorous and unoriginal observation: the typical viewing habits of most, at this point in history, are cursory at best. The amount of visual content that we are subjected to through our internet usage practically demands swift thoughtlessness: otherwise we would all keel over trying to figure out the cultural and personal ramifications of some Honey Boo Boo gif. Or, maybe not. Regardless, the decision to dedicate time and quality brain waves to digital content, can feel burdensome, but in the rare instances when one loses their self in time and viewing, the sense of burden is replaced with startling wonder.

Digital video artists are thus posed with the question of how to seduce or drag someone into their fabricated realm long enough for them to swirl it around in their mouth, spit it out, and then have it swim in the back of their mind for the rest of the hour (or if lucky, the rest of their life), sometimes declaring that it smacked of aged oak, sometimes wondering if it existentially shook them.

In his Pink Face Series, Ben Ehrmann answers this question with a soft and vulnerable nakedness, the whites of his eyes and the blacks of his pupils jutting out against the pink paint that covers his body, the floor, and the walls. The digital recordings of Ehrmann's performances hardly look like Facebooklive events, nor any other ShapChat/Instagram/what have you video content—instead they demand that you wonder what they actually are, what the portrayed character is up to. He's not selling anything, he's not telling you about his new morning workout routine and how best to do push-ups, he's not telling you about the amazing, high-fiber smoothie he made just this afternoon. He's not really telling you anything at all and he's hardly even asking for your attention.

Instead, the character recalls one of Beckett's, someone who doesn't appear to know why he's doing what he's doing, but knows for sure that he is doing it and will keep on doing it, until perhaps, he stops doing it. And so, a viewer who spends time with the Pink Face Series will look at a pink painted man putting on lipstick from the vantage point of a mirror, they will see him covering himself in pink paint and breaking eggs on his body. Viewers will watch him hopscotching through piles of canvas stretchers, blowing pink bubbles and popping pink balloons. To some extent, these acts seem equal to one another, Ehrmann's face revealing very little about the emotional experience of the activities, as if in each instance we were simply witnessing an animal approaching a self-assigned task for the mere purpose of stubbornly carrying it out.

Sitting through the series, a viewer may begin to uneasily wonder, what is the difference between this pink painted man banging his head on the wall and myself, mindlessly plucking out chin hairs in front of the mirror late at night? What is the difference between myself and this man who doesn't quite seem to know why he's doing what he's doing but insists on doing it anyway? At that point, a viewer may mosey away from the screens displaying Ehrmann's performances, but later imagine themselves akin to that pink man staring into space and wonder exactly what it is they themselves are doing and why they are doing it.

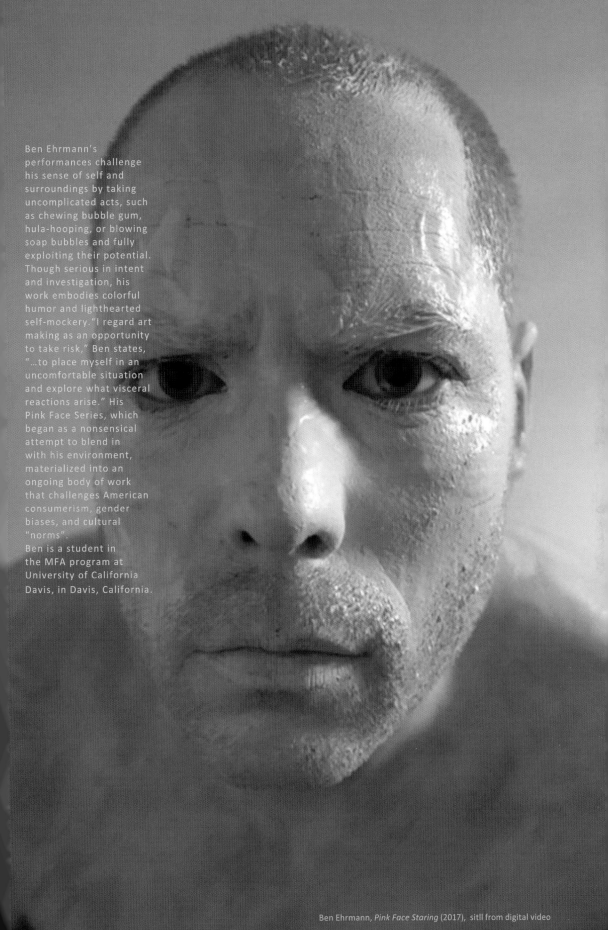

Ben Ehrmann's performances challenge his sense of self and surroundings by taking uncomplicated acts, such as chewing bubble gum, hula-hooping, or blowing soap bubbles and fully exploiting their potential. Though serious in intent and investigation, his work embodies colorful humor and lighthearted self-mockery. "I regard art making as an opportunity to take risk," Ben states, "...to place myself in an uncomfortable situation and explore what visceral reactions arise." His Pink Face Series, which began as a nonsensical attempt to blend in with his environment, materialized into an ongoing body of work that challenges American consumerism, gender biases, and cultural "norms".
Ben is a student in the MFA program at University of California Davis, in Davis, California.

Ben Ehrmann, *Pink Face Staring* (2017), sitll from digital video

66

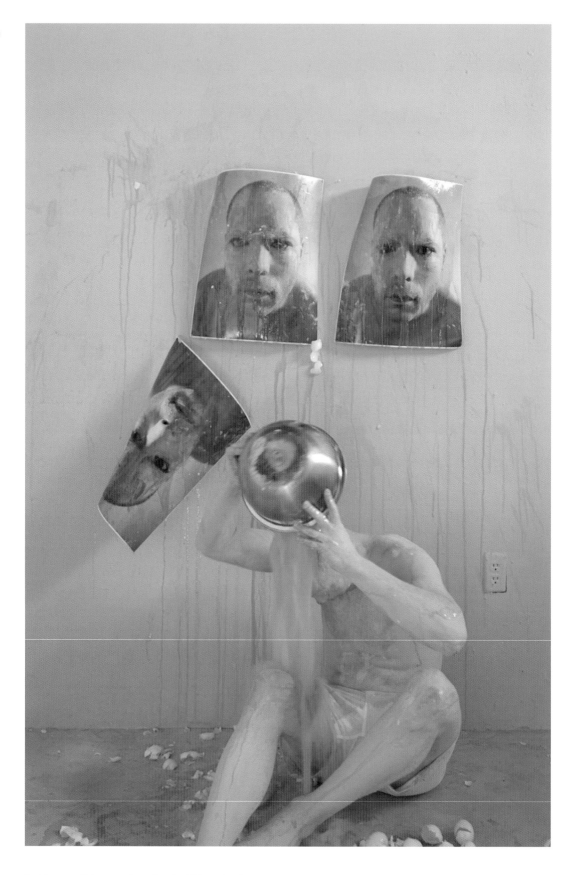

Ben Ehrmann, *Pink Face and Eggs* (2017), sitll from digital video

매력적이지 않고 독창적이지 않은 관찰: 역사상 현시점에서 대부분의 전형적인 관람 방식들은 기껏 해봐야 호기심이다. 우리가 인터넷 서핑을 통해 받아들이는 수많은 시각적 정보들은 사실상 우리에게 신속한 부주의함을 요구해. 그게 아니면 우리는 짤 (Honey Boo Boo gif)의 문화적 및 개인적 파급력에 압도되어 버리겠지. 아니면, 아닐 수도 있고. 그럼에도 불구하고, 당신의 시간과 고퀄리티 두뇌를 디지털 콘텐츠에 바치기로 한 결정은 부담이 됐겠지만, 덕질에 자신을 잃어가는 시간이 드물게 부담감에서 놀라운 경이감으로 바뀌기도 한다.

이런 이유로 디지털 비디오 아티스트는 관람객들을 유혹해서 가상의 영역으로 오랫동안 머물게 함으로써 그들의 입안에 오래 빙빙 돌고 뱉어진 후, 그 이후에도 몇 시간 (또는 운 좋게는 평생) 그들이 다시 그 속으로 뛰어들 수 있게 어떻게 만들 수 있을까 고민한다. 그것은 그들의 중요한 무언가를 건드리거나 존재적으로 그들을 건드리는 무언가가 있어야 가능할 것이다.

Pink Face Series에서 Ben Ehrmann 작가는 그의 드러난 부드러운 알몸, 그의 몸과 바닥, 벽을 뒤덮은 핑크색 페인트 너머로 드러난 하얀 흰자위와 검은 눈동자를 통해 이에 대한 대답을 던진다. Ehrmann의 퍼포먼스는 페이스북 라이브 이벤트 같지도, 아니면 다른 스냅챗, 인스타그램과 같은 비디오 콘텐츠 같지도 않다. 대신, 영상은 관람자가 그것이 무엇인지 궁금하게 만들며, 묘사되는 주인공이 뭘 할 것인가를 궁금하게 만든다.

대신, 그의 캐릭터는 그가 뭘 하는지도 왜 하는지도 모르는 것 같이 보이지만 그가 하고 있고 계속할 거라는, 또는 그가 멈추기 전까지는 계속할 거라는 사실은 확실히 알고 있는 듯하다는 점에서 베케트 (Beckett)를 회상하게 한다. 그런 이유로, Pink Face Series를 관람하는 누구든 거울이 잘 보이는 위치에서 립스틱을 바르는 분홍 페인트칠 된 남자를 보는 데 시간을 보낼 것이며, 그가 분홍 페인트를 뒤집어쓰고 달걀을 자기 몸으로 깨뜨리는 모습을 보게 될 것이다. 관람자는 그가 캔버스 더미 사이에서 뛰어 놀고, 핑크색 풍선껌을 불고 터트리는 모습 또한 보게 될 것이다. 어떤 점에서 이런 행동들에는 공통적인 특징이 있다. Ehrmann의 얼굴은 거의 감정을 표현하고 있지 않은데 그것은 마치 우리가 자신의 주어진 임무를 다하겠다는 일념으로 이를 묵묵히 이행하는 동물을 바라보고 있다는 느낌이 들게 한다.

이 시리즈를 바라보면서 관람자는 핑크색으로 뒤덮은 이 남자가 벽에 자신의 머리를 치는 모습과 한밤중에 턱에 난 털을 무념무상으로 뽑는 자기 자신이 무엇이 다른가에 대한 거북한 질문을 던진다. 그가 하는 짓을 왜 하는지 모르지만 계속해야만 하는 그와 내가 무엇이 다른 걸까? 그 시점에서 관람자는 Ehrmann의 퍼포먼스 영상이 설치된 스크린에서 느릿느릿 걸어 나가겠지만, 그 이후 전시실을 노려보고 있는 핑크맨과 자신이 닮았다는 것을 느끼며, 그가 무엇을 하고 왜 하는지에 대해서 생각해 볼 것이다.

Joy Miller 저

Ben Ehrmann는 퍼포먼스를 통해 풍선 껌을 씹거나 훌라후프를 하거나 비누 거품을 가능한 한 크게 부는 등의 복잡하지 않은 행위를 취함으로써 자신과 주변에 대한 자신의 감각에 도전한다. 의도와 조사에 진지함으로 일관하지만, 그의 작품은 다채로운 유머와 가벼운 자기 조롱을 포함한다. Ben은 "예술을 위험을 감수하는 기회로 간주한다"라고 정의하며, ".... 내 자신을 불편한 상황에 처하게 하고 원초적인 반응이 무엇인지 탐구한다." 라고 덧붙였다. 그의 환경에 적응하기 위한 비논리적 시도로 시작된 '핑크 얼굴 시리즈 Pink Face Series'는 미국의 소비주의, 성적 편견 및 문화적 "규범"에 도전하는 작품으로 구체화되며 진행되고 있다. Ben은 캘리포니아 주 데이비스에있는 University of California Davis의 순수미술 석사 프로그램 학생이다.

Ben Ehrmann, *Wall* (2017), sitll from digital video

KUN FANG

How can I prove am I a HUMAN?
And when am I a machine?? love machine!!
When do I feel and touched like human? Or
I touched the machine to feel I just touched
the human body ?
Why do we need love???
Or love need us?
Do we really need love to be more human.
There are 38 kind of love.
Is love a word or is words love?
Who is the finder of love?
Is a body? Or is a soul? Or is it nothing?? or
it is a virus.
What is LOVE?
Is all about feelings and nuances ?
About what we feel.
But.....

What make us live and feel lived.
Or is just dead and just dead fresh
yesterday????

How can we prove that we are living?
How can we prove that we are dying ??
There still dead walking in the palace of the
shadow
sweet empathy
words. code.
Every images need its words to said
To improve they have had a soul.

Every object who made by its imperfections

Are made already in the mind.
In the creativity of the human hands
Crazy like hell.

They have all been in the processing of
emotions of the
Maker.
And they are out the divine hands. They all
already exigencies the mind of the maker. Or
better to said in the hand
Of something high intelligence allowed they
can have their own
Destiny.
This journey of the erotized seed of body
and soul is alive
Like the madness of the mad mad professor
who created female Frankenstein.
Want to live with her forever.
This is made love sounds priceless and
horrible.
Processable!?

What I need is a beautiful strawberry.
My machine body need
To pro the first bite.
And I still have some good flavor over in me.
Love is consumable

Teased like Pierre Marcolini

And feel the flesh body
Full of hormones
It is blood. tears. and
Sweat.
It is not the t shirt of the visible
convergence.
It is not top art.
It is not working.
not just materials.
It is in the brain.
The brain consuming the flesh.
And everything what we can see or not
can see. touch or not can touch
Everything have their right to be here
And we can made it happen just like the
mad mad professor
Live and dead with our creatures

What is sex?
When am I women?
When am I man??
When am I both???
Do I really need my nipples??
Do man really need its penis?
We are already not just human anymore!!

I don't know when I can see him. And
where?
Me and my virtual lover
I am dancing with my voice!.
I don't care .
I do not care about my future!
If love is a virus .do we really need future??

Even don't know am I living or dying?
In data.
Dreaming living and sleeping dying
in data . And my flesh and blood in data.
I'm so scared . Because passion is not data!
It is bitter and about feelings.
I'm weak and ......

It is about nothing.
Why do we need words to said about the
art??
How do I express this in my messages to the
Data I like??

I m scared because
Is this cyber aura.
The life were documented
By pictures.
Even words is not just words anymore
The data explain it to us!!
online.

Feel.
We are living with our digital data. More and
more I feel live like machine!

When am I a human?

Kun Fang, *Milk and Honey,* still from digital video

내가 사람이라고 어떻게 증명할 수 있
을까?
내가 언제 기계일 수 있을까??
난 기계가 너무 좋아!
내가 언제 사람처럼 느끼고 만질 수 있
을까? 혹은
기계를 만진 다음 인간의 몸을 만졌다고
느끼기 위해서일까?
왜 우리는 사랑이 필요하지?
혹은 사랑이 우리를 필요로
하는 것일까?
우리가 더 사람다워지기 위해 정말로 사
랑이 필요할까?
38가지의 사랑이 있어.
사랑이 하나로 표현이 될까
아니면 표현하는 게 사랑일까?
사랑을 찾는 이는 누구인가?
몸인가? 영혼인가? 아니면 아무것도 아닌
가?? 그것도 아니라면 그저 하나의 바이
러스인 것일까.
도대체 사랑이란 무엇일까?
감정과 의미의 미묘한 차이가
그것의 전부일까?
우리가 느끼는 것들 말이야.
그런데...

무엇이 우리를 살게 하고 우리가 살아있
다고 느끼게 하는가.
혹은 죽었거나 어제 방금 죽은 걸까.

어떻게 우리가 살아 있다는 것을 증명할
수 있을까?
어떻게 우리가 죽어가고 있다는 것을 증
명할 수 있을까?
그림자의 궁전에는 아직도 죽은자들이
걸어 다녀.
달콤한 공감
단어. 코드.
모든 이미지는 그것을 말하기 위한 단어
가 필요해.
그들이 영혼을 가지고 있다는 것을 발전
시키기 위해서라도.

각각의 불완전함을 가지고 만들어진 모
든 오브제는

이미 마음속에서 만들어져 있어.
사람 손의 독창성 안에서
정말 미친 일이야.

그들은 모두 감점을 처리하는 경험을 가
지고 있어.
그리고 그들은 신성한 손으로부터 탄생
했어. 그들은 모두 이미 위급함을 경험한
적이 있어. 혹은 그들이 그들 자신의 운
명을 가질 수 있도록 허락된 어떤 높은
지능을 가진 손안에 있다고 말하는 게
나을 수도.
이 여행은 에로틱한 씨앗의 몸 그리고 살
아 있는 영혼의 것이야.
여성 프랑켄슈타인을 창조한 정신 나간
교수의 광기와 같이.
그녀와 평생을 함께 하고싶어.
이것은 무시무시하고 값을 메길 수 없는

Kun Fang, *Milk and Honey,* stills from digital video

사랑의 소리로 만들어진 것.
과연 가공할 수 있을까?
나에게 필요한 건 아름다운 딸기.
내 기계적인 몸이 완벽해지기 위한 그 첫 한 입.
그리고 여전히 내 전신에 적셔 있는 그 맛있음.
사랑은 소비적인 것이야.

Pierre Marcolini처럼 놀림 받았어.
그리고 그 육체를 느껴봐
하모니로 가득 찬
이것은 피. 눈물. 그리고
땀.

이것은 단지 시각적으로 가리기 위한 옷이 아니야.
이것은 고급 예술도 아니고, 일도 아니며 단순히 질료도 아니야.
이것은 뇌 속에 있어.
엄청나게 강렬한 조직, 뇌
그리고 우리가 볼 수 있는 또는 볼 수 없는 것의 모든 것.
만질 수 있는 것 또는 만질 수 없는 것이지.
모든 것들은 이곳에 있을 수 있는 그들만의 권리를 갖고 있어.
그리고 우리는 마치 그 미치광이 교수처럼 그것이 일어날 수 있도록
만들 수 있지.
우리가 만든 생명과 함께 살거나 죽거나.

섹스란 뭐야?
언제 난 여자이며
언제 난 남자이며
언제 난 둘 다 일 수 있지?
나에게 정말 젖꼭지가 필요할까?
남자들은 정말 그들의 생식기가 필요할까?
이미 우리는 더 이상 그냥 인간으로 존재할 수 없어!!

나는 그를 언제 그리고 어디서 볼 수 있을지 몰라.
나와 나의 가상의 애인
나는 내 목소리와 함께 춤을 추고 있어.
상관없어.
난 내 미래에 대해 전혀 걱정하지 않아!
만약 사랑이 하나의 바이러스라면, 우리에게 미래란 필요한 것일까??

심지어 내가 죽어가는 건지 살아가고 있는지조차 모르겠어.
데이터 안에서.
꿈을 꾸며 살고 잠을 자며 죽지
데이터 안에서. 그리고 데이터 속의 나의 살과 피.
난 너무 무서워. 왜냐면 열정은 데이터가 아니거든!
이것은 격렬함 그리고 감정에 관한 것.
나는 약하고 그리고...

이건 아무것도 아닌 것에 관한 거야.
왜 우리는 예술에 대해 말할 때 단어가 필요하지?
어떻게 하면 표현할 수 있을까
이것이 내가 좋아하는 데이터에게 보내는 나의 메시지라는 것을?

난 무서워 왜냐하면
이것은 가상의 아우라이기 때문이야.
인생은 사진에 의해 기록 되어졌어.
심지어 단어도 이제 더 이상 그냥 단어가 아니게 되었어.
그 데이터가 그것을 우리에게 설명해주지!!
온라인.

느껴봐.

우리는 우리의 디지털 데이터와 함께 살고 있어. 점점 더 점점 더 내
가 기계와 같은 삶을 산다는 것을 느껴!
내가 언제 인간일 수 있을까?

Kun Fang was born in 1974 in
Beijing, China. Since 1990 she lives
in Belgium. In 2000 she graduated
from the Royal Academy in Antwerp.
The story of Kun Fang's video is
about seduction in the digitale age.
The digital body create the unique
feeling only imagined not felt by
the other. And the romantic data
become a journey.

Kun Fang은 1974년 중국 베이징에서 태어
났다. 1990년 이후부터 그녀는 벨기에에서
살고 있다. 2000년 그녀는 Antwerp 로열
아카데미에서 졸업했다
Kun Fang의 영상 작품은 디지털 시대의
유혹에 관해 다룬다. 디지털 육체는 타자를
통해 느낄 수 없는 독특한 감정을 불러일으
킨다. 로맨틱 데이터는 새로운 여정이 된다.

EONA JIAWEI GAO

Finding Dreamlands, Finding Myself

By Eona Jiawei Gao

Building an identity lies along a path of dreams, and the ultimate treasure is self-realization. To me, self-identification is a reflection of the world that we live in. When we talk about "the world", we are actually talking about our autognosises. Talking about "the world" or "the things in the world" is a process expressed through our personal views. It is a way to explore ourselves.

I had many questions about myself, and sometime these questions deeply depressed me. I questioned the things I saw. Just because I saw them which were the reflections of the world in my mind, it, the reflections in my mind, did not mean that they really existed in the world. They were what my brain had processed. Essentially, they were "results", but I wanted to see the original world. I was questioning "the world", but I was simultaneously questioning who I was.

In *A New Poem* (2015), I put my questions to the public. For instance, when I was learning English, I compared it with my mother tongue, and I wondered whether when people called something "pink", it exactly matched the color "粉红" in my native language. I have not gotten the answer, but there is one thing I am 100 percent sure of: that there are 100 different shades of pink among 100 different people who say "pink". Language is a "result", and I want to know the original meaning. In *A New Poem* (2015), I broke Emily Dickinson's *If I Can Stop One Heart from Breaking* into many words, which were read by many people. Those people must have different thoughts, although they are reading the same thing. It is very hard to know their personal reactions to Dickinson's poem, but I know that the thoughts in their minds when they are reading the poem, are different from the thoughts in Dickinson's mind when she was writing it.

If language did not exist, could I see the real world? If my brain stopped working, what information would I receive? If the words in poems did not have meanings, or if my brain did not assign meaning to those words, the things I would receive would be tunes. This would be much like listening to a strange language. I recall an occasion in which my Italian friend was talking on the phone to his family. I did not know what he was saying, but I found his voice to be more appealing than usual. I paid more attention to his voice, gestures and emotion, and found they composed a beautiful moment. Another time, when I was in a room, I asked other people what color the wall was. Someone said it was white, but I saw it as pink. My brain cried, "It is white!" But in the real world, it was pink; the wall was reflecting the light pink glow of the sunset. I find the world without the "meanings" to be very vivid. If we can see a dreamland without being aware of it, can we see ourselves without self-awareness? What would we see? I desire to realize my identity. Putting away awareness may be the process to complete myself; this is the reason I am here.

The rise of these salfie is particularly interesting within this context. The selfie is common now, but it is still new. I first discovered selfies about 15 years ago because of the rise of digital cameras, camera phones and the Internet/social networking. These conditions intermingled: digital cameras digitized photos, which could be easily stored and copied; cellphones with cameras made it easier for anyone to take photos anywhere, anytime. And finally, social networking, the most important element,

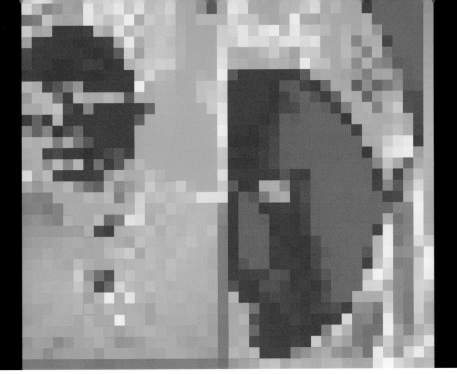

Sorry... I was worried.

Wait, so you told her I'm back?

created demand for tons of selfies. Thus, the selfie has become a part of our daily lives. Around the same time selfies were blossoming, I was forming my personal consciousness. These preconditions helped accelerate the process of building my self-identification. I do not know whether the prior generations had their own version of the "selfie", but I find traces in portraits, photos and biographies. Self-identification can be found in various forms throughout history.

I'm trying to put away my self-identification in my selfie. *Talia* (2017) is a video portrait about a selfie without an identity, yet in truth, it is full of self-awareness. Two girls are talking about asking Talia something, but by reciting the dialogue, viewers will find that they themselves are Talia, and she is making a call to herself: Talia is asking Talia to call Talia for something, and then Talia calls Talia to ask Talia something. It is a "repeating" call to herself. It is like a selfie–a one-man show performed by only one person. It should be full of self-awareness, but viewers will easily lose the awareness of self, because "Talia" does not show her identity when she is talking to herself; she is pretending to speak with someone else.

Talia (2017) is an experiment. Before it, I also did some other tests, including *I Am You* (2016), which was inspired by my daily life. I found that people prefer to enforce their personal wills on other people, animals and things. For instance, we name pets and dress them, but we do not know whether they need this. In *I Am You* (2016), I directly placed my head on a mannequin, and let the mannequin be me. It looked as if I was trying to move awareness of myself to the mannequin, but it was actually showing how we use our strong self-identifications. In another experience, when my friend was watching me paint, I used a mirror as the painting's base and let him watch before I finished it. I thought he would watch the image for a while, and then give me a critique, but he did not. He spent much more time watching himself through the image – the mirror. He expressed his self-identity through watching my painting process. It was a very interesting experience.

The way we watch the world is the way we watch ourselves. When we have self-awareness, the things we see are like the mirror, which reflects ourselves, instead of the real world. I am seeking to lose awareness while I am in this world, and going to see if there is a dreamland beyond what we see here. In the process, I am finding my identity, which hides behind my own self-awareness.

N.Y., Apr 25, 2017

Eona Jiawei Gao, *Talia* (2017) , still from digital video

꿈의 장소를, 내 자신을 찾아

Eona Jiawei Gao

정체성을 구축하는 것은 꿈을 따라감에 있으며, 궁극적으로는 자아를 실현하는 것이다. 나에게 있어 자아 인식은 우리가 살고 있는 세계에 대한 반영이다. 우리가 "세상"에 대해 이야기할 때, 우리는 사실 본인들의 자기 인식에 관해 이야기한다. "세상" 혹은 "세상의 것들"에 관해 말하는 것은 개인적인 견해를 표현하는 과정이다. 결국, 자기 자신을 탐험하는 하나의 방식이다.

나는 스스로에 대해 많은 질문을 던졌고 가끔 그 질문들이 나를 우울하게 만들었다. 나는 내가 본 것들에 대해 질문했다. 내가 본 것들은 내면이 투영된 것뿐, 내면에 비친 모습이 실제로도 세상에 존재한다는 것을 의미하지는 않는다. 그것들은 내 머리속에서 일어난 일들이다. 근본적으로, 그것들은 "결과"였지만 나는 원형의 세계를 보고 싶었다. "세계"에 질문함과 동시에 나는 내가 누구인지 질문하고 있었다.

A New Poem (2015)에서 난 대중에게 질문했다. 예를 들어 내가 영어를 배우고 있을 때, 사람들이 핑크색 - "pink"라고 부르는 것과 "粉红"의 색이 정확하게 일치하는지 궁금했다. 답을 얻지는 못했지만, 100% 확신할 수 있는 한 가지가 있다. 100명의 사람들에게 100가지의 각기 다른 "Pink"가 있다는 것이다. 언어는 "결과"이며, 나는 근본적 의미를 알고 싶다. *A New Poem* (2015)에서, 나는 에밀리 디킨슨의 "*내가 만일 하나의 마음이 여러 단어로 부서지는 것을 멈출 수 있다면*"이라는 많은 사람에게 읽힌 시의 개념에 도전했다. 사람들은 똑같은 것을 읽지만 각기 다른 생각을 가지고 읽는다. 디킨슨의 시를 읽은 개개인의 반응을 아는 것은 매우 어렵지만, 시를 읽고 있을 때 마음속에 떠오르는 생각은 디킨슨이 시를 적던 때의 감정과 의도와는 분명 다를 것이다.

언어가 없다면 현실 세계를 볼 수 있었을까? 뇌가 멈추면 어떤 정보를 받을 수 있을까? 시의 단어가 의미가 없거나 뇌가 단어에 의미를 부여하지 않으면 내가 얻을 것은 그저 음에 불과하다. 이는 마치 이상한 언어를 듣는 것과 같을 것이다. 이탈리아 친구가 전화로 가족과 이야기하던 때가 생각난다. 어떤 이야기를 하는지 몰랐지만 그 목소리가 평소보다 더 매력적이라 생각했다. 그의 목소리, 몸짓, 감정에 더 많은 관심을 기울였고, 그의 모든 행동이 순간의 아름다운 찰나로 지나갔다. 또 언젠가 방에 있을 때, 다른 사람에게 벽이 어떤 색인지 물어봤다. 하얀색이란 답이 돌아왔지만 나에게는 분홍으로 보였다. 뇌가 소리쳤다, "하얀색이야!" 그러나 현실에서는 벽이 일몰의 연분홍빛을 반사하고 있었으니 현실에서는 분홍색이었다. 나는 "의미"가 없는 세계가 매우 생동감 있다는 것을 알게 되었다. 꿈을 꿔도 꿈이라고 인지하지 못한다면, 우리가 스스로에 대한 자각 없이 자신의 모습을 볼 수 있을까? 우리는 무엇을 보게 될까? 나는 내 정체성을 깨닫고 싶다. 인식하지 않는 것이 나 자신을 완성시키는 과정이 될 수도 있다. 이것이 내가 여기 있는 이유다.

이러한 맥락에서 셀피의 등장은 상당히 흥미롭다. 지금은 셀카가 흔한 게 돼버렸지만, 아직 새로운 것이다. 디지털카메라, 카메라 휴대폰, 인터넷과 SNS의 등장으로 약 15년 전 처음 셀카를 알게 되었다. 셀피에는 여러가지 복합적 조건이 있다: 디지털 카메라는 디지털 사진을 쉽게 저장하고 복사할 수 있게 해줬고, 사진 기능이 있는 핸드폰으로는 언제 어디서든 쉽게 사진을 찍을 수 있게 해주었다. 마지막으로 가장 중요한 요소인 SNS가 수많은 셀카에 대한 수요를 창출했다. 이런 흐름 속에 셀카는 우리 일상의 일부가 되었다. 이렇게 셀카 문화가 꽃필 그 무렵, 나는 자의식을 형성하고 있었다. 이런 문화는 내가 자의식을 구축하는 데에 도움이 되었다. 이전 세대도 그들 나름의 "셀카"를 가지고 있었는지 알 수 없지만, 초상화, 사진과 자서전이 같은 맥락에 있을 것이다. 자아 인식은 역사를 통해 다양한 형태로 발견될 수 있다.

나는 셀카를 통해 자아 인식하려는 것을 그만두려 한다. *Talia* (2017)는 정체성이 없는 셀카에 대한 비디오 초상화이지만 사실은 자기 인식으로 가득 차 있다. 두 소녀가 탈리아에게 무언가를 부탁하는 것에 관해서 이야기 하지만 대화 내용을 보면 그 두 소녀가 바로 탈리아라는 것을 알게 될 것이다. 탈리아가 그녀 자신에게 전화를 거는 장면에서 탈리아는 탈리아에게 전화해 탈리아에게 무언가 부탁하고, 탈리아는 탈리아에게 전화를 걸어 탈리아에게 무언가를 물어봐 달라 부탁한다. 이는 탈리아 자신에게 회귀하는 "반복되는" 전화. 마치 한 사람이 혼자 원맨쇼 셀카를 보여주는 것과 같다. 이 원맨쇼는 자기 인식으로 가득 차 있어야 하지만, 관객은 이 사실을 잊기 쉬울 것이다. 왜냐하면 "탈리아" 는 자신과 대화할 때 자신의 정체성을 보여주지 않고 타인과 대화하는 척하기 때문이다.

Talia (2017)는 하나의 실험이다. *Talia* (2017) 이전에도 일상생활에서 영감을 얻은 *I Am You* (2017)를 포함한 몇 가지 시도가 있었다. 나는 사람들이 타인들과 동물, 사물에 그들의 개인적 의지를 강요하고 싶어 한다는 것을 발견했다. 예를 들어 우리는 애완 동물에게 이름을 지어주고 옷을 입혀주지만 정작 동물이 원하는 가에는 관심이 없다. *I Am You* (2016)에서 나는 마네킹에게 내 머리를 병치해서 마네킹이 나인 것처럼 두었다. 마치 내가 마네킹에게 나의 자아 인식을 옮기려고 하는 것처럼 보였지만 사실은 우리가 어떻게 강한 자아 정체성을 사용하는지 보여준다. 또 한번은 나는 거울에 그림을 그런 적이 있었는데 채색이 끝나기 전에 친구에게 보여주었다. 그 친구가 한동안 내 작품을 보고 피드백을 줄 것으로 생각했지만 그는 그러지 않았다. 그보다 그는 거울을 통해 자신을 지켜보는 것에 더 많은 시간을 보냈다. 그 친구는 내가 그림을 그리는 과정에서 자신의 정체성을 표현했다. 이는 매우 흥미로운 경험이었다.

우리가 세상을 보는 방식은 우리 자신을 보는 방식이다. 우리가 자기 인식을 가질 때, 우리가 보는 것들은 거울과 실제 세상을 보여주는 대신 거울같이 우리 자신을 비춘다. 나는 이 세계에 있는 동안 인식에서 벗어나 우리에게 보이는 것 너머에 이상의 세계를 찾을 것이다. 이 과정에서 나는 나 자신의 인식 저편에 숨어있는 내 정체성을 찾을 것이다.

2017년 4월 25일 뉴욕

Eona Jiawei Gao is a New York-based artist and designer. She received a BA in Animation from Beijing Institute of Fashion Technology and an MFA in Interactiver Arts from Pratt Institute. Since 2010, she started the digital video works, and related experiments. She mainly works on the digital image, video, interactive installation and performance. Most of her work experiences presenting the relationship of time and space, and reveals her intimate thoughts about this world. Eona Jiawei Gao cares about the translation of her thoughts, and position of audiences. She presents what she have seen and thought about through different lens – a visible way and a deep reflection, which brings a strong view to spectators.

Eona Jiawei Gao는 뉴욕에 기반을 둔 아티스트이자 디자이너다. 그녀는 북경 패션 기술 연구소에서 애니메이션 학사 학위를 받았으며 Pratt Institute에서 Interactive Arts 석사 학위를 받았다. 2010년부터 디지털 비디오 작품 및 관련 실험을 시작했다. 그녀는 주로 디지털 이미지, 비디오, 인터렉티브 설치 및 공연 작업을 한다. 대부분의 작업은 시간과 공간의 관계를 보여주며 이 세상에 대한 그녀의 속 깊은 생각을 보여준다. 작가는 자신의 생각이 해석되는 것과 독자의 입장, 두 충돌에 대해 고심한다. 그녀는 새로운 렌즈를 통해 시각적이고 깊은 자아 성찰이 담긴 강한 강렬한 장면으로 그녀가 경험하고 생각한 것을 표현한다.

INBAR HAGAI

The inner world of Foot Stretcher

By Danielle Kaganov

Inbar Hagai's first documentary is a "becoming" project. The film describes the director's effort to become a ballerina despite the lack of physical aspects - her age (21) and lack of gymnastic skills. The director's statement is: I will enter a strict training regiment, the ballet will become my whole life and no matter what I will become a ballerina. With this promise the film enters into motion, with a plot that was developed during the year and a half of shooting the film combines between documentary scenes of ballet lessons, interviews with key figures from the local ballet scene, staged fantasy, and collages of found footage from the Internet.

While this plot line might seems to have the characteristics of an episode from MTV's "Made" this basic plot structure is only an outline of a wider narrative. Hagai serves the audience a reflective view into the psychological and ethical mechanisms those "transformation shows" employ.

Why do we as viewers enjoy these shows? Do these shows reflect the way we look at the real world? Why are we attracted to the process of transformation from ugliness into beauty? Why are those before and after images of extreme physical transitions evoke in the viewer a state of longing and anticipation, in a similar vein of pornography?

My perspective on the film come from within it's creation process. I joined the creation process halfway through as the film's editor. While the film indicates a long self-learning process of the non-theoretical aspects of movie making that took over two years of shooting and editing... I came into this project without prior experience and gained new knowledge from it. During the long and often gruelling process I perfected my editing skills. The editing process included the creation of many different rough cuts between the numerous shooting days. This process culminated after the shooting process was completed with the re-editing of must of the material into one final cut. By that point the editing became more loyal to the essence of Inbar as a character in the film and less loyal to the events that occurred during her try to become a ballerina.

Inbar started the project during her second year of studying in art school she finished it during her fourth and final year. During this time the project became almost another life , like some kind of alternate reality that became intertwined with the creator's real life. The film became an extension of the creator's self and psyche embodying inside it all the different promises that the creator wished to achieve. I came to know two different women - one of the immediate reality and one from the imaginative reality of the film and the two lived together blended and blurred all at once.

This film exists on the osculation point of these two realities. On the one hand it's clear that the film is a biographic work embodying the creator's personal history and psychological inclinations of violence and self-destruction. On the other hand the unsentimental and un-nostalgic narrative of the film with it's almost no use of pathos creates a pathetic aura that embodies the film's main heroine allowing the viewer to feel empathy to the protagonist.

The personal biography and the basic instincts serve as a basis for key questions about filmmaking, watching rhythm, the story and the narrative as well as the general meaning of art.

So if it's here... Hold on, breathe.

Inbar Hagai, *Foot Stretcher* (2017), stills from digital video

Foot Stretcher 의 내면 세계

Danielle Kaganov

Inbar Hagai의 첫 번째 다큐멘터리는 "점점" 발전하는 프로젝트이다. 이 영화는 신체적 조건이 부족함에도 불구하고 발레리나가 되기 위한 감독의 노력을 묘사한 것으로, 그녀의 나이 (21세)와 체조 기술 부족이 큰 관건이었다. 감독의 성명은 다음과 같다: 나는 엄격한 훈련에 참여할 것이며, 내가 어떤 발레리나가 되던 발레는 내 인생 전체가 될 것이다. 이 약속을 영화는 시작되고, 1년 반의 촬영 기간에 걸친 발레 수업과 현지 발레계의 주요 인물과의 인터뷰, 무대에 서는 것 같은 환상, 인터넷에 있는 영상들의 콜라주가 병치되며 영화는 진행된다.

이 각본 라인이 MTV의 "Made" (10대가 목표를 이루는 과정을 보여주는 리얼리티 쇼) 에피소드의 특성을 갖는 것처럼 보일 수도 있지만 이 각본 구조는 더 넓은 서사의 개요일 뿐이다. Hagai는 청중에게 "인생역전 쇼"가 제공하는 심리적, 윤리적 메커니즘에 대한 반성의 시각을 제공한다.

왜 시청자는 이런 쇼를 즐길까. 이 쇼는 우리가 현실 세계를 보는 방식을 반영할까. 왜 우리는 추함에서 아름다움으로 변모하는 과정에 끌릴까. 왜 극단적으로 변하는 몸의 전후 이미지가 시청자들에게 포르노그래피와 비슷한 맥락처럼 기대감을 불러일으키게 할까.

영화에 대한 내 견해는 영화 제작 과정에 있다. 난 제작 과정 중간 즈음 영화 에디터로 참여했다. 이 영화는 2년간의 촬영과 편집을 거친 비전통적 방식의 습득 과정을 담고 있는 중...나는 이 프로젝트에 사전 지식 없이 들어갔다. 길고 때로는 지독한 과정에서 편집 기술을 완벽하게 다듬었다. 편집 과정은 방대한 촬영본에서 러프 컷을 잘라내면서 진행된다. 이 과정은 촬영 과정이 끝난 이후 파이널 컷으로 쓰기 위한 영상 재편집과 함께 완료됐다. 그 시점에서 편집은 발레리나가 되기 위한 시도들보다는 영화 주인공 Inbar의 본질을 담아내는 데에 더 충실해졌다.

Inbar은 미술대학에서 2학년으로 공부하는 중 이 프로젝트를 시작했고, 4학년 마지막 학기에 이를 끝마쳤다. 이 기간 동안 프로젝트는 제작자의 실제 생활과 얽혀있는 일종의 대체 현실과 같은 또 다른 삶이 되었다. 이 영화는 그녀가 기록

하고자 했던 자기 자신과 그녀의 마음의 연장선에 있다. 나는 두 명의 다른 여성을 알게 됐다. 하나는 현실의 그녀이고 하나는 상상력으로 만들어진 현실의 그녀이다. 둘은 함께 살았고, 섞이며 모호해졌다.

이 영화는 두 현실의 접촉 지점에 존재한다. 한편으로 제작자의 개인사와 심리적 폭력성과 자기 파괴적 성향을 구현한 자서전적 작품임이 분명하다. 한편 냉담하고 비(非)노스텔지어적 서사와 파토스 (pathos: 청중에 감성을 호소하는 것)를 거의 사용하지 않는 영화는 관객이 주인공에게 연민을 느낄 수 있는 분위기를 연출한다.

개인사와 인간의 기본적 본능은 영화 제작, 감상의 흐름, 이야기와 서사 및 전반적 예술의 의미에 대한 핵심 질문의 근간이 된다.

Inbar Hagai, *Foot Stretcher* (2017), stills from digital video

Born at 1992 in Kfar-Saba, Inbar Hagai is a young artist and filmmaker. She was a recipient of Alieen Cooper prize from Bezalel Academy at 2015, and of a supporting grant from Rabinovich Foundation at 2016. Her art documentary film, "Foot Stretcher", was featured at DocAviv Film Festival (Tel Aviv, May 2017), The 3rd International Exhibition on New Media Art, "Digital Body," CICA Museum (South Korea, May 2017) and in New Media Film Festival (L.A., June 2017). Hagai's works have been exhibited in Palermo Gallery (Stuttgart) and the CICA Museum (South Korea). Her latest work, "Christian" was presented at Manifesta 11 in Zurich.

1992년 Kfar-Saba에서 태어난 Inbar Hagai는 예술가이자 영화 제작자이다. 그녀는 2015년 Bezalel 아카데미에서 Alieen Cooper 상을 받았고, 2016년 Rabinovich Foundation으로부터 보조금을 지원받았다. 그녀의 다큐멘터리 영화 "Foot Stretcher"는 DocAviv Film Festival (Tel Aviv, May 2017), 제3회 뉴 미디어 아트 국제전: 디지털 바디, CICA 미술관 (한국, 2017년 5월), 뉴 미디어 영화제 (L.A.m 2017년 6월)에서 주목 받았다. Hagai의 작품들은 Palermo Gallery (Stuttgart), CICA 미술관에서 전시되었다. 그녀의 가장 최근 작품 "Christian"은 스위스 취리히에 있는 Manifesta 11에 전시되었다.

MARY HANLON

Violence towards women in film lives in every genre from every decade. *It's only a movie.*

Our violence is fetishized, tied up in a bow, buried in contradictions and happy endings.

It soups from stereos in hypnotic melodies, loitering in our subconscious for an indeterminate period. It is draped in couture and handed smooth golden statues, minimized because it exists within the boundaries of entertainment. Its perpetrators are not all stereotypical, one-dimensional bad guys, but rather presidents, Hollywood legends, comedic geniuses, style icons. Men other men aspire to be.

In the infancy of moving images, many prophesized the effects they would have on the human psyche. In the 1859 *Atlantic* article *The Stereoscope and the Stereograph*, Oliver Wendell Holmes commented that the experience of viewing a film was, "as if reality had lost its own continuous connection and had become shaped by the demands of our soul."

In Stanley Kubrick's *A Clockwork Orange*, Alex says, "It's funny how the colors of the real world only seem real when you viddy them on the screen," after he undergoes Ludovico's technique, where he is injected with nausea inducing drugs and forced to watch graphically violent films.

The Veritas Technique is a reflection of this malady of our culture, boiled down to its purest state, undressed and vulnerable. By removing sequences of violence against women from the narrative cause and effect chains of their original films and juxtaposing them with examples across genres and decades, this artwork aims to overwhelm the senses in an attempt to lift the veil; remove the filters.

Mary Hanlon, *The Veritas Technique* (2016), Installation stills

The Veritas Technique (진리 요법)

영화 속 여성을 향한 폭력은 모든 시기 모든 장르 속에 존재해 왔다. *단지 영화일 뿐이잖아.*

폭력은 대상화되고, 리본으로 묶이고, 모순과 해피 엔딩으로 묻혔다.

아는 몽롱하게 만드는 멜로디 속에서 활기를 띠며 모호한 상황에서 무의식 안에서 맴돈다. 폭력은 엔터테인먼트라는 명목으로 최소화되어 멋진 맞춤옷으로 입혀진 황금 동상으로 관객에게 선보여진다. 가해자들은 모두 틀에 박힌 일차원적 나쁜 놈이 아닌, 오히려 대통령, 할리우드의 전설들, 코미디 천재들, 패션 아이콘들이다. 남자들의 워너비 그 모습으로.

초기 영화가 발명될 무렵 학자들은 영화가 인간의 정신에 미칠 영향에 대해 많은 예측을 했다. 1859년 아틀란틱지의 기사 *The Stereoscope and the Stereograph*를 보면, Oliver Wendell Holmes는 영화 관람에 대해 이렇게 언급했다. "마치 현실이 자신만의 연결 고리를 잃고 우리 마음이 원하는 대로 형태를 갖추는 것 같다."

스탠리 큐브릭 감독의 *A Clockwork Orange*에서 주인공 알렉스는 폭력적 성향 치료를 위해 어지러움을 유도하는 약물을 투여받고 폭력적인 영화를 강제로 보게 하는 루도비코 요법을 받게 된다. 그 후 그는 "현실의 색이 촬영한 영상으로 볼 때 얼마나 더 생생한지 놀라울 따름이다"고 말한다.

*The Veritas Technique*는 우리 문화의 병폐를 반영하고, 벗겨지고 취약한 가장 순수한 상태로 정제한다. 여성을 향한 폭력적 장면을 영화의 서사 구조와 인과관계에서 끊어내고 다른 장르 영화들의 비슷한 장면들과 나란히 병치함으로써 이 작품은 감각적 압도감으로 가려져 있던 면들을 드러내는 데에 목표가 있다.

Mary Hanlon is a new media artist, filmmaker and writer. She is currently pursuing her MFA at Hunter College's Integrated Media Arts program in New York. She is a graduate of the Riggio Honors Writing and Democracy program at The New School, has been a contributing writer for The Brooklyn Rail and Girls Against God, and was the recipient of the MacDowell Colony fellowship in 2014. Mary worked as a model and moved on to study method acting before enrolling at the New School in 2007. A mix of media, gender and feminist studies nudged her vision into focus, allowing her to synthesize a chaotic passage through the film and fashion industries with her creative endeavors. Mary's work is driven by a need to identify and question aversion towards women in the media. She currently lives in Brooklyn, and works as an art director.

Mary Hanlon은 뉴 미디어 아티스트이자 영화 제작자 및 작가이다. 그녀는 뉴욕에 있는 Hunter College의 통합 미디어 예술 프로그램에서 석사 과정을 밟고 있다. 그녀는 the Riggio Honors Writing and Democracy 프로그램을 The New School에서 졸업했으며 The Brooklyn Rail과 Girls Against God에 참여 작가였고 2014년 the MacDowell Colony의 장학금 수상자였다. Mary는 모델로 일했고 2007년 the New School에 입학하기 전까지 연기를 배우기 위해 계속 전진했다. 영화와 패션계의 혼란스러운 여정 속에서 매체와 젠더, 페미니스트 연구는 그녀를 집중할 수 있게 해주었고 집대성할 수 있게 해주었다. Mary의 작업은 대중 매체 속에서의 여성 혐오를 발견하고 의문을 던지게 만든다. 그녀는 현재 브루클린에 거주하며 아트 디렉터로 일하고 있다.

Mary Hanlon, *Frenzy*

MAGGIE HAZEN

Embodied Imaginary:

From Gendered Bodies in Virtual Spaces to Powerful Bodies in a Physical World

by Maggie Hazen, 2016

The ways in which we imagine the technologies of the future can speak volumes about our concern in the present. More specifically, we might say that prospective techno-scientific advances illuminate the perceived horizons of political possibility. How might we intervene within these developments in order to articulate a more emancipatory future, free from perceived gender and sexuality norms? We are always in the act of becoming something else, and technological mediation makes this even more so. Virtual bodies, cyborg bodies, and queer bodies promise un-fixed identities. But who is in control of these bodies? Are they controlled by a fiction we author via action cinema, video games, war narratives? The future we speculate about is uncertain and open for change. We must be careful of the mythologies and narratives we construct through technology as they will inevitably schematize our designs for a post-human future. In massive multiplayer online role-playing games (MMORPGs) a person can create an avatar completely distinct from one's self. These interactive virtual environments enable real-time interaction with fictional, visual landscapes. Such uncertain spaces propose a fiction that originates in the imagination—constructing a hybrid space where the virtual self becomes the real self. Here, people play out their desires to become different versions of themselves. Very often, it is the masculine, militant superhero and warrior characters performed in virtual spaces that serve as place-holders until other versions of selves can be developed. It is these often violent characters that are constructed and integrated into the physical body.

Literary critic Katherine Hayles defines "virtuality" as "the cultural perception that material objects are interpenetrated by information patterns." Virtuality is associated with computer simulations that put the body into a feedback loop with a computer-generated image. However, in full-immersion VR, one perceives being physically present in a non-physical world. The degree to which the virtual or artistic environment consistently reproduces reality determines the degree of suspension of disbelief. The greater the suspension of disbelief, the greater the degree of immersive presence achieved. Recent developments in virtual technology and software have accelerated the fluidity between control and response movements in video games to such an extent that the distinction between the real and the virtual has begun to collapse. In video game environments, gamers' physical bodies are not fully immersed in an environment but can be connected to the virtual by fingertips, arm movements, eye movements, voice, and other sensory organs to the extent that the mind embodies a virtual organism. Gamelike simulators used by the US Army root the virtual in reality. In 2014, Army News Service announced that the future of the US Army's training environments will feature live holistic synthetic combat training, which integrates various simulations into a single, remotely accessible system. Enemy jets will be piloted from a thousand miles away by soldiers, some in aircraft simulators and others on computer gaming stations. Gaming is not yet officially part of the Army's simulation syllabus but is expected to be soon. The sensory distinction between the virtual and the real is certainly becoming thinner, which has obvious consequences for "players" mistaking the real for the virtual and vice-versa.

It is essential to consider how we are gendering technology and aim to actively shift the conversation we are currently imagining around speculative fictions and other narrative worlds. The virtual environment must not construct its critical edifices upon an uninterrogated mythologization of gender and sexuality as they stand, but rather remake the world as we wish to see it. Such reimagining could reshape our technopolitical future.

Maggie Hazen, *HULK* (2016), still from digital video (top), _ (middle, bottom)

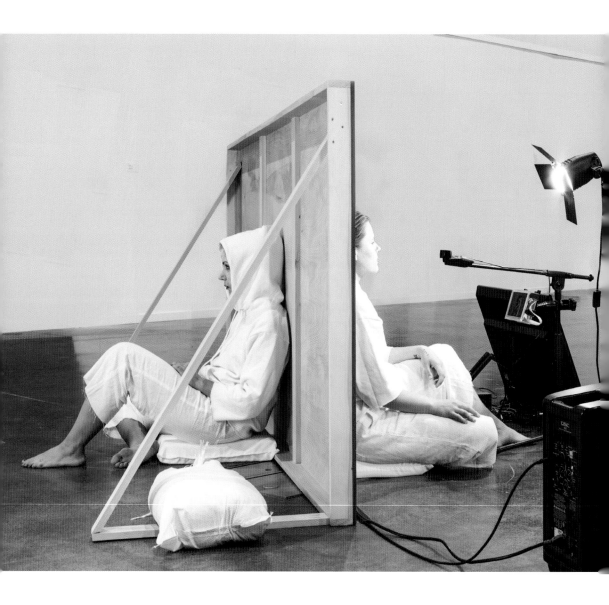

Maggie Hazen

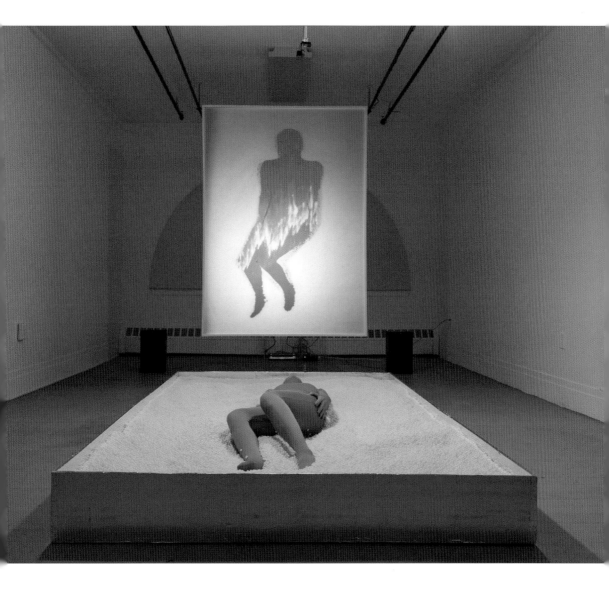

Maggie Hazen

체화된 상상:
가상 공간의 성적인 육체로부터 현실 세계의 강한 육체까지

Maggie Hazen, 2016

우리는 미래 기술에 대해 상상하며, 미래 기술이 현 문제들에 대해 해결책을 제시할 수 있다고 생각한다. 더 구체적으로, 도래할 기술과학적 진보가 정치적 가능성의 지평을 열어 줄리라는 것이다. 성 역할과 성 정체성으로부터 해방된 미래를 위해 우리가 어떠한 방식으로 이러한 발전에 개입할 수 있을까? 우리는 언제나 다른 무언가가 되는 과정에 있으며, 기술의 도입은 이를 가속화한다. 가상의 몸과 사이보그 몸, 그리고 성 소수자의 몸은 가변의 정체성을 지닌다. 그러나 누가 이러한 신체들을 통제하는가? 액션 시네마, 비디오 게임, 전쟁 서사를 통해 저자들에 의해 제어되고 있는가? 우리가 예측하는 미래는 불확실하며 변화의 가능성이 있다. 우리는 기술을 통해 신화와 서사를 구축할 때 좀 더 신중할 필요가 있다. 이는 신인류의 미래를 위한 원형이 될 것이기 때문이다. 온라인 롤플레잉 게임 (MMORPG)에서 사용자는 자기 자신과 완전 별개의 아바타를 만들 수 있다. 이 참여형 가상 환경은 허구적인 세계와 실시간으로 상호 작용할 수 있게 해준다. 불확실한 공간은 상상에 기반을 둔 허구를 만들어 내며 가상의 자아는 현실의 자아가 되는 혼합 공간이 구축된다. 흔히 가상 공간에서 주인공은 남성적인 군사 영웅이나 전사이며 그들은 다른 버전의 주인공이 개발되기 전까지 사용자 자신의 대체자가 된다. 육신으로 구축되고 실현되는 것은 보통 이러한 폭력적인 캐릭터다.

문학 비평가 Katherine Hayles는 "가상"을 "물질적인 대상이 정보 패턴에 의해 관통되는 문화적 인식"이라고 정의한다. 가상 세계는 신체를 컴퓨터가 만든 이미지와 반복된 피드백으로 연결하는 컴퓨터 시뮬레이션과 관련이 있다. 그러나 완전몰입 가상 현실에서는 사용자가 비물리적인 세계에 물리적으로 존재하는 것처럼 인식한다. 가상 또는 예술 환경이 지속해서 현실을 재현하는 수준이 불신의 유예 정도를 결정한다. 불신하려는 마음이 머뭇거릴수록 몰입감의 정도가 커지는 것이다. 가상기술과 소프트웨어의 최신 발전으로 인해 비디오 게임의 제어와 동작의 응답이 자연스러워지면서 현실과 가상의 차이가 붕괴하기 시작했다. 비디오게임 환경에서 게이머의 신체는 가상환경에 완전히 몰입되지 않지만, 손가락 끝, 팔 움직임, 눈동자의 움직임, 음성 및 기타 감각 기관을 가상에 연결할 수 있다. 미 육군이 사용한 게임 같은 시뮬레이터는 현실에 기반을 둔 가상이다. 2014년 미 육군 보도관은 다양한 전투를 하나의 원격 제어 시스템으로 통합한 통합 전략 시뮬레이션 훈련을 미 육군에 도입한다고 발표했다. 적 제트기는 군인이 수천 마일 떨어진 곳에서 항공기 시뮬레이터와 컴퓨터 게임 스테이션을 통해 조정될 것이다. 게이밍은 아직 공식적으로 미군 시뮬레이션 강의에 포함되어 있지 않지만, 곧 포함될 전망이다. 가상과 현실 간의 감각에서 느껴지는 차이는 확실히 얇아지고 있고, 결국 이는 '플레이어'가 가상으로 만들어진 현실과 그 반대의 경우도 마찬가지로 착각하게 할 수 있는 결과를 가져올 것이다.

우리가 어떻게 기술을 성으로 양분화되고 있으며 우리가 상상해내는 허구와 스토리의 세계에 관한 적극적인 담론이 시급하다. 가상 공간은 성과 정체성에 대한 관념들을 고민 없이 그대로 반영해서는 안 되며 우리가 원하는 방향으로 구축해야 한다. 이러한 상상력은 우리의 기술 정치적 미래를 바꾸어 놓을 것이다.

Maggie Hazen (b.1989) is a New York-based artist born and raised in Southern California. Hazen is an interdisciplinary artist working in sculpture, video and performance. She holds an MFA from the Rhode Island School of Design and a BFA from Biola University in Los Angeles. She has done collaborative research at CERN, MIT and Brown University. Her work considers and critiques the representation of history, place, and the self within the structures of power encompassing our physical and digital worlds. Her solo exhibitions include Brown University's Granoff Center (2016); and the Los Angeles Museum of Tolerance (2012) for the 20th anniversary of the 1992 LA Riots. Her past exhibits include, OBO at Microscope Gallery, Brooklyn, NY (2016); and The Boston Young Contemporaries, Boston, MA (2014). Most Recently she studied at the European Graduate Studies in Switzerland to research art and estrangement where she also exhibited her work. Her residencies have included Vermont Studio Center (2016) and a collaboration with Pasadena Side Street Projects (2014). Hazen teaches at Bard College in the department of studio arts and experimental humanities.

Maggie Hazen (b. 1989)는 뉴욕 기반 예술가로, 남부 캘리포니아에서 태어나고 자랐다. Hazen은 조각, 비디오 및 퍼포먼스 분야에서 다양하게 작업하는 예술가이다. 그녀는 the Rhode Island School of Design에서 석사를 로스엔젤레스에 있는 Biola University에서 학사를 취득했다. 그녀는 CERN과 MIT, Brown University에서 공동 연구를 진행했으며 그녀의 작업은 우리를 물리적 및 디지털 세계를 포괄하는 권력 구조 내에 역사와 장소 및 자아의 표상들에 관해 다루며 비판한다. 그녀는 Brown University의 Granoff Center (2016)와 1992년 로스앤젤레스 폭동 20주년을 기념하는 Los Angeles Museum of Tolerance (2012)에서 개인전을 가졌다. 또한 뉴욕 브루클린 Microscope Gallery의 OBO (2016)와 매사추세츠 보스턴 The Boston Young Contemporaries (2014) 전시에 참여했으며, 최근에는 스위스 the European Graduate Studies에서 예술과 소외에 관해 연구했으며 전시회를 했다. 그녀는 Vermont Studio Center (2016)과 Pasadena Side Street Projects (2014)에서 레지던시를 했으며 현재 Bard College의 스튜디오 예술학 및 실험인 문학과에서 학생들을 가르치고 있다.

PETER HRISO

Peter Hriso, *Pears 3*

In my work there are no messages or hidden agendas, other than to reveal the discoveries made during my investigations. There is a seed of an idea or a bit of a plan when I begin, but I am quickly directed by the work, answering the needs, sorting the puzzles and discovering solutions through the aid of technology. I use food and still lives as a springboard for my personal expression. It is a classical subject matter with a long history that has become somewhat of a cliché. Nonetheless, I enjoy the juxtaposition between digital and nature.

내 작품은 어떤 메시지도, 숨겨진 의제도 없으며, 내 연구에서 발견된 보여줄 뿐이다. 나는 아이디어의 씨앗이나 약간의 계획으로 작품을 시작하지만, 작업이 시작되면 작업이 나를 이끈다. 필요한 것을 찾고, 퍼즐을 맞추고, 기술을 통해 해결책을 발견하며, 음식이나 정물을 개인적 표현의 발판으로 삼는다. 고전적 주제이고 다소 진부할 수도 있지만, 그럼에도 나는 디지털과 자연 사이의 병치를 즐긴다.

Peter Hriso, *Cherries*

Peter Hriso has been an artist and animator now for over twenty years. He has worked in various positions and is currently an Associate Professor of Art, the Chair of the Department of Art and Director of Digital Animation at Missouri Western State University. He teaches graduate and undergraduate courses in animation and design.

Peter Hriso는 예술가이자 애니메이터로 20년이 넘게 활동했다. 그는 여러 가지 직책으로 근무했고, 현재는 미주리주 서부 주립 대학에서 교수이자 예술학부의장 그리고 디지털 애니메이션 디렉터로 역임하며 애니메이션 및 디자인 대학원 및 학부 과정을 가르치고 있다.

DANIEL JOHNSON

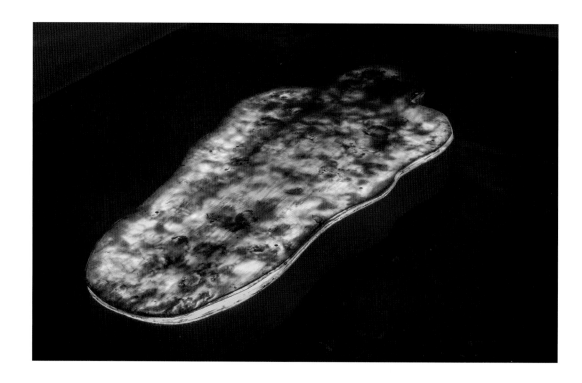

Daniel Johnson, *Shroud* (2016)

"The word as experience belongs to the basic word I-It. The basic word I-You establishes the world of relation." (Martin Buber, I and Thou)

Our imprints are everywhere, in our interactions with the landscapes, communities, and environments we inhabit. By imagining the future, we can begin to see how our actions leave a mark, a trail of breadcrumbs leading back to a choice, an observance, or neglect.

I and Thou, by Martin Buber, Touchstone, New York, 1996

Shroud

2016, Installation using encaustic paint on layers of plexiglass, and other mixed media

A meditation on diversity within a landscape.

"경험으로서의 단어는 기본단어 나-이것 I-IT에 속한다. 기본단어 나-너 I-You는 관계의 세계를 구축한다." (Martin Buber, I and Thou)

우리의 흔적은 우리가 살고 관계를 맺는 풍경, 사회, 환경 모든 곳에 있다. 미래에 대한 상상으로 우리는 우리의 행동이 어떤 흔적을 남기는지, 의식하는 삶과 게으른 삶에 대한 선택이 남길 자취를 볼 수 있다.

I and Thou, Martin Buber 저, 뉴욕 터치스톤, 1996년.

수의

2016년, 플렉시 유리 층에 납화법 (밀랍을 녹여 만든 그림물감을 사용하는 기법)을 사용해 만든 설치물.

풍경의 다양성에 대한 명상.

Balloon (Confessions)

2015, Installation using expended air from my lungs, balloons, string
I blew up several balloons, filling them with air from my lungs. I then arranged the balloons into a sar-
cophagus like figural form. Over time the air I expended into the balloons will leak away, destroying
the form, and releasing the air into the outside world. This work is a meditation on my own limits, my
relationships with others, and how my actions will outlast my bodily presence in the universe.

풍선 (고백)

2015년, 직접 분 풍선을 줄로 설치.

내 폐를 통한 공기로 풍선을 채운 후 석관 모양으로 배치했다. 시간이 지남에 따라 공기를 불어 넣은 풍선은 바람이 빠
져 형태가 무너지고, 숨은 밖으로 나갈 것이다. 이 작업은 나 자신의 한계와 나와 타인과의 관계에, 나의 행동이 어떻
게 우주에서 나의 육체적 존재를 넘어설 수 있는가에 대한 매개물이다.

Daniel Johnson, *Balloon (Confessions)* (2015)

Daniel Johnson is a mixed-media artist currently based in Tucson, Arizona; where he earned a Master of Fine Arts at Southwest University of Visual Arts. Born in Kansas City, Missouri in 1987, he attended College of the Ozarks in Point Lookout, Missouri, earning a Bachelor of Arts in Computer Art. His work has been included in exhibitions throughout the United States and abroad. Most notably, his work was included in the 2015 Arizona Biennial at the Tucson Museum of Art, curated by Irene Hoffman, Phillips Director and Chief Curator of Site Santa Fe. He was an Honorable Mention in the 11th Semiannual Competition of the Dave Bown Projects, juried by Curators Katherine Pill of the Museum of Fine Arts, Ron Platt of the Grand Rapids Art Museum, and Kelly Shindler of the Contemporary Art Museum St. Louis. Additionally, he was featured in Expose Art Magazine's 2016 Next Generation of Artists competition and in Studio Visit Magazine, Volume 29 and 36. Internationally, he is slated to exhibit his work at the Czong Institute for Contemporary Art Museum in Gimpo, South Korea in 2017. His expanded studio practice explores conceptions of consciousness, semiotics, interconnectivity, longing, mortality, and becoming in the ecology of culture. He is a free spirit and nomad, chasing the horizon.

Daniel Johnson은 현재 애리조나주 투손에서 활동하는 혼합 매체 아티스트이다. Southwest University of Visual Arts에서 석사 학위를 취득했다. 1987년 미주리 주 캔자스 시에서 태어난 그는 미주리 주 포인트 룩아웃의 University of the Ozarks에서 컴퓨터 예술 학사 학위를 받았다. 그는 투손 미술관에서 Irene Hoffman과 필립스 디렉터, 사이트 산타페 현대미술관 수석 큐레이터가 주관한 2015년 애리조나 비엔날레에 참여하는 등 국내외에서 작품을 발표하였다. 그는 Museum of Fine Arts의 Katherine Pill, Grand Rapids Art Museum의 Ron Platt, 그리고 St. Louis의 현대 미술관의 Kelly Shindler이 심사하는 Dave Bown 프로젝트의 11번째 대회에서 장려상을 받았다. 또한 Expose Art Magazine 29권 2016년 차세대 아티스트 공모전과 Studio Visit Magazine 36권에 실리며 주목을 받았다. 국제적으로 그는 김포의 Czong 현대 미술관에서 2017년 그의 작품을 전시할 예정이다. 그는 의식, 기호학, 상호 연결성, 갈망, 죽음에 대한 개념을 탐구하고 문화의 생태계에 대해 연구한다. 그는 자유로운 정신을 가진 방랑자로서 지평선을 쫓고 있다.

KEVIN H. JONES

For many years your studio practice centered on painting. When and why did you move from painting to digital art?

This all happened when I started to use silkscreens when creating my paintings. I purchased a Power Macintosh 6100 around 1995 to make the artwork for the silkscreens. Soon I was laying out painting compositions on the Macintosh. I could also go back to the time when I first viewed *The Way Things Go* by Peter Fischli and David Weiss and studio critiques with Paul McCarthy. *The Way Things Go* showed me that I didn't need to illustrate natural phenomena but I could employ it in my work. Paul McCarthy stressed that my work could become much more interesting if it was time-based or sculptural. I heeded his advice and never looked back.

What are the concepts surrounding some of your most recent work?

The investigation of our relationship to the natural word continues in my work. Most recently I have been looking at various representations of the "laboratory" that span paintings from the 17th century to contemporary labs. The paintings from the 17th century such as David Teniers II, *Interior of a Laboratory with an Alchemist,* depict a workspace just as the title indicates. An alchemist is working in a domestic space that is filled with not only his apparatuses but also familiar items from daily life. Science at that time was not practiced in a sterile space but in a kitchen or spare room. I like how that matter-of-fact quality portrayed in these works contrasts the institutionalized laboratory we're accustomed to today. Although, I am not sure how these "settings" for laboratories will manifest in my work.

Other subjects that have been contemplated are conjuring vs. science in recent work. Science seeks the truth whereas magic/conjuring seeks to deceive us.

Would you call some of your work absurd?

Absolutely. The use of the absurd in my work personifies our futile attempts to understand the natural world and the cosmos. I think it is necessary to not only add humor to the work but also a since of bewilderment.

You have been included in two exhibitions at the CICA Museum this year. First is *Objectified* and the second is *The Digital Body*. Could you talk about the work exhibited in these exhibitions?

The video work, *Placebo #3*, that is in *Objectified* looks at aspects of truth, deceit, and concepts of beauty. The female body builder posing juxtaposed with the voice over, sets up an almost instructional ambiance. This feeling of conclusiveness quickly fades once we realize that the voice over is about chance and the ephemeral.

Concerning Things That Can Be Doubted #1 that was part of *The Digital Body* is a more meditative video project. Building upon the structure of the periodic table with fragmented images include: a woman blowing kisses, a hand playing rock paper scissors, and an ice cube melting. All of which are in a cluster. Other moving images such as candles burning at both ends and hands creating shadow puppets orbit around these central images. Meaning fluctuates in this work from seduction, disembodiment, and then eventuate to a sense of loss.

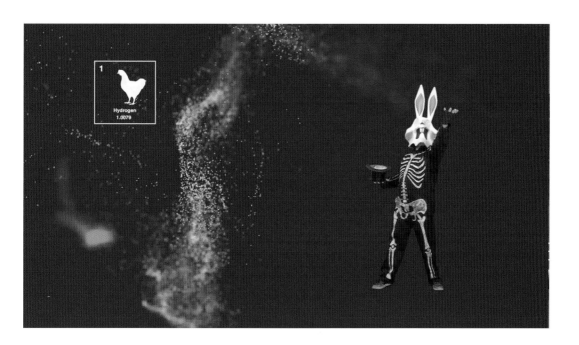

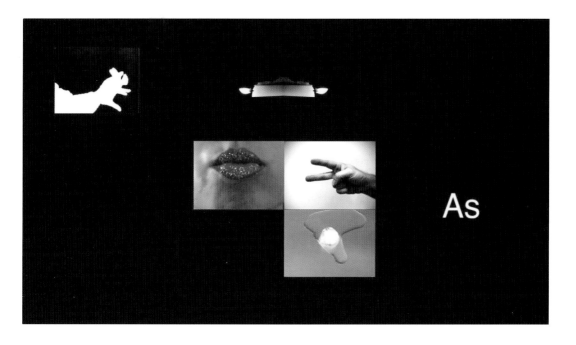

Kevin H Jones, *Placebo #2* (2013) still from digital video (top),
Concerning Things That Can Be Doubled #1 (2016), still from digital video (bottom)

수년 동안 회화 중심으로 작업했었다. 언제, 왜 회화에서 디지털 아트로 전향했나?

실크스크린을 시작하면서부터이다. 1995년 실크스크린을 위한 삽화를 만들기 위해 파워 매킨토시 6100 컴퓨터를 구매했다. 그 후 컴퓨터를 사용해 그림을 구성하기 시작했다. 또한 Peter Fischli의 에세이 *The Way Things God*와 Paul McCarthy의 스튜디오 평론에도 영감을 받았다. *The Way Things Go*에서 내가 자연 현상을 묘사할 필요 없이 내 작업에 이용할 수 있다는 것을 알았다. 또한, Paul McCarthy는 내 작업이 시간 기반이거나 조각으로 표현된다면 훨씬 더 흥미로울 것 같다고 조언했고 나는 그의 의견에 동의해 작품을 전향하게 되었다.

최근 작품에 영향을 준 개념들이 있다면 무엇인가?

단어와 인간의 관계에 관심이 있다. 가장 최근에는 17세기부터 현대에 이르는 다양한 그림들을 찾아보며 "실험실"의 다양한 대표성에 대해 관찰했다. 예를 들어 17세기 터너의 *Interior of a Laboratory with an Alchemist*라는 회화 작품은 제목 그대로 작업 공간을 묘사했다. 연금술사는 실험 도구뿐만이 아닌 생활 도구로 가득 찬 실내 공간에서 일하고 있다. 그 당시의 과학은 독립된 공간이 아닌 주방이나 남는 방에서 연구되었다. 성실하게 묘사된 당시 장면과 현대의 제도화된 실험실과 어떻게 다른가 살펴보는 것은 흥미롭다. 비록 실험실에 대한 나의 연구가 내 작업에 어떻게 반영되는지는 불확실하지만 말이다.

또 관심 있는 주제는 마술과 과학에 대한 차이이다. 과학은 진실을 추구하지만, 마술은 속이는 것을 추구한다.

본인의 일부 작품이 엉뚱하다고 생각하나?

물론이다. 내 작품에 담긴 부조리함은 자연 세계와 우주를 이해하려는 우리의 헛된 시도를 보여준다. 나는 작업에 유머를 더할 뿐만 아니라 당황스러움도 담아낼 필요가 있다고 생각한다.

올해 CICA 박물관 전시회에 두 차례 참가했다. 첫 번째 전시는 *Objectified*이고 두 번째는 *The Digital Body*이다. 이 전시회에 전시된 작품에 관해 이야기해 줄 수 있나?

*Objectified*에서 소개된 영상 작품 *Placebo #3*은 진리와 속임수, 미의 개념에 대해 다룬다. 음성과 함께 자세를 취하는 여성 보디빌더는 교육적 분위기를 연출한다. 이러한 확신은 음성이 끝나면서 함께 사라진다.

*The Digital Body*에서 전시된 *Concerning Things That Can Be Doubted #1*은 좀 더 명상적인 영상 작업이다. 주기율표와 함께 키스를 보내는 여성, 가위바위보를 하는 손, 녹는 얼음 큐브 등의 이미지 파편들이 조합된다. 모든 요소은 하나로 엮여서 보여진다. 그리고 양 끝이 타고 있는 양초와 그림자 인형을 만드는 손 영상은 이를 공전한다. 의미는 유혹과 이탈, 그리고 손실의 감정으로 변화한다.

현재 루이지애나의 뉴올리언즈에 살고 있는 Kevin H. Jones은 Virginia Commonwealth 대학에서 회화 및 판화과를 졸업하고, 어스틴의 텍사스 대학에서 회화 전공으로 석사 학위를 받은 후, 예일 대학에서 디자인으로 다시 석사 학위를 받았다.

지난 4년간 Kevin은 회화, 비디오, 물리적 컴퓨팅, 그리고 최근에는 2D 디지털 프린트 등 여러 매체를 복합적으로 다루고 있다. 매체 혼합을 이용해 도표, 도식 및 시스템으로 자연을 표현하려는 그의 연구는 그의 작품을 관통하는 주제이다. 초창기에는 태양 에너지를 에너지원으로 사용하는 허구의 방송국에 관한 작업을 했으며, 최근에는 센서를 이용한 인터렉티브 비디오 설치를 통해 예측 불가능성에 관한 질문을 던진다.

Kevin은 미국, 아시아 그리고 유럽 등지에서 전시를 진행했다. 또한, 그의 작업은 ID Magazine, Idea Magazine, Neural Online, The New York Times, MSNBC 등에 실렸다. 최근에는 일본 도쿄의 Art Lab AKIBA, 시드니의 Stasjon K, 도쿄의 Ginza Geijutsu Laboratory, 리치먼드 1708 Gallery에서 전시를 열었다.

최근 Kevin은 2011-2012년 Board of Regents ATLAS grant 수상, 2009-2010년 같은 해 루이지에나 레지던시에서 The Louisiana Division of the Arts Artist Fellowship 선정, 2008년 노르웨이 산네스의 AIR 레지던시 선정, 2006년 Houston Contemporary Art Museum 에서 KAT 기금을 받았고 1995년과 2000 년에는Virginia Museum of Fine Arts Fellowship에 선정되었다.

그는 그린즈버로의 노스 케롤라이나 대학, 오리건 대학, 펜실베이니아 대학에서 학생들을 가르쳤으며 현재는 툴레인 대학의 the Newcomb Art 과에서 교수로 역임 중이다.

Kevin H. Jones currently resides in New Orleans, Louisiana. Kevin has degrees from Virginia Commonwealth University (BFA, Painting and Printmaking), The University of Texas at Austin (MFA, Painting) and Yale University (MFA, Design).

Over the past four years within Kevin's work, one can see transitions in and synthesis of media including painting, video, physical computing, and more recently, 2-dimensional digital prints. Through this synthesis of media, the conceptual investigation of the natural world through charts, diagrams and systems is a constant theme. His early work used solar energy to power a fictional television station, while more recent work uses sensors to create an interactive video installation that questions entropy.

Kevin has exhibited throughout the United States, Asia and Europe and his work has been featured in ID Magazine, Idea Magazine, Neural Online, The New York Times and MSNBC. Most recently, he has exhibited his work at Art Lab AKIBA in Tokyo Japan, Stasjon K in Sandnes, Norway ,Ginza Geijutsu Laboratory in Tokyo, Japan and 1708 Gallery in Richmond VA.

Kevin was recently awarded Board of Regents ATLAS grant 2011-2012, The Louisiana Division of the Arts Artist Fellowship for 2009-2010; the Louisiana ArtWorks, Studio Residency Program 2009-2010; AIR, Residency, Stasjon K, Sandnes, Norway 2008; the KAT Fund, Houston Contemporary Art Museum 2006 and two Virginia Museum of Fine Arts Fellowships 1995, 2000.

He has taught at The University of North Carolina at Greensboro, The University of Oregon, The University of Pennsylvania and currently is an Associate Professor in the Newcomb Art Department at Tulane University.

Kevin H Jones, *Concerning Things That Can Be Doubled* (2013), still from digital video

NORMAN KLEIN & MARGO BISTIS

"The Double Object of The Imaginary 20th Century"

by Norman M. Klein & Margo Bistis

The Imaginary 20th Century is a comic historical novel, written by Norman M. Klein and Margo Bistis, and published by the media museum ZKM. With a team of artists, the authors have constructed a unique narrative engine to unfold a story in which facts and fiction, history and legend, split off and return to each other. The viewer accompanies the characters across two centuries, and three continents.

According to legend, in 1901, a young woman named Carrie, while traveling in Europe, selects four men to seduce her, each with a version of the coming century. Inevitably, the future spills off course. We navigate through the suitors' worlds; follow Carrie on her misadventures; witness what she and her lovers forgot to notice. Gradually we find out that Carrie's life is implicated in her uncle's world of business and political espionage. For over forty years, Harry Brown was hired by oligarchs to erase crimes that might prove embarrassing. Thus, as he often explains, espionage is a form of seduction.

Harry is a kind of lock-box. His clients assumed that he could bury anything, at least that was his legal guarantee. That promise is challenged in 1908 when Carrie shoots a man in New York while embroiled in anarchist politics. Luckily, the crime never goes to trial. Other scandals follow, inspiring Harry to begin an archive about his niece's world in 1917. It was also Harry's way of visiting his niece by proxy—even if she wasn't' there (which was often). Being very modern, Harry liked to build efficiencies. People, like information or electricity, should be at his convenience.

The archive operated literally by machine. Gears on tracks pushed along cards in metal sleeves. Thousands of documents could be rolled backwards, forwards, and sideways. The device was built at a shipyard. It steered mostly in two directions: first as a novel of seduction; and second as a codex for espionage.

The Imaginary 20th Century mobilizes a vast digital archive of 2,200 rare images, early films, a series of voice-overs, interactive maps, and spaces designed for the viewer to navigate. Featuring an exploratory interface, the data narrative (www.imaginary20thcentury.com) prompts interactivity of a kind that resembles an archaeological excavation. Viewers dig through movable, layered assemblages of image-cards, embedded into chapter maps, each with their own soundscape. The maps are about place, but also function as mappae-mundi revealing the state of mind for that part of the story. Voice-over narration reveals key moments of the story, but also leave gaps, suggesting what the makers of "Carrie's archive" decided to leave out.

The card design speaks to the ubiquity of printed cards in the era before World War I. The card was an essential tool for sociability—the cabinet card, the postcard--; for home entertainment—the stereocard—; for libraries and archives—the card catalogue; for government—the census machine--, and for data processing in business. Punched cards for tabulators existed long before computers.

The historical research on the period from 1893 to 1925—the setting of the story-- was very broad-based, focusing particularly on the city, the body, industry and technology, imperialism, wars and social movements. This research entailed a back-and-forth process, moving between story development and collection building, between authoring and curating. "Carrie's archive" incorporates old and new media circa 1900, harvesting its content from period illustration, cartoons, photography, film, industrial design, architectural drawing, science fiction, fantasy, and utopian novels, medical texts, and more. The archive's development into a data narrative has relied upon a contrapuntal mix of visual and print media. Texts and visual objects together tell the story.

The name for such a contrapuntal mix of technology and culture was famously coined in 1816. In a letter of that year, the German philosopher Friederich Schelling described seeing a novel moving like a water clock, inside a great hall. He called it a 'wunder-roman'. Traditionally, a wunder-roman only makes

The Imaginary 20th Century (2016), Image cluster of the data narrative

sense if crucial parts of its story are missing. The missing pieces are said to have inspired machina (mental pictures). In the eighteenth century, these machina usually held engravings and movable puppetry. A wunder-roman often hides clues to an amoral order. It is a picaresque of unfinished business. For Harry's part, he became obsessed with progress that never got built, except as fiction—the half-eaten shapes that are misremembered fifty years later: fishtailed blimps and insect helicopters. Progress blows off course.

The missing pieces of data narrative of *The Imaginary 20th Century* inspired the writing of the novel and the essays. A separate component of the unfolding engine of fact and fiction, the print book is independent but essential to the full measure of the tale. Here, the authors no longer rely purely on what Harry has left us. Researching beyond Harry's version of things, the novel reveals clues to Carrie's world that Harry decided to leave out. It takes readers into Carrie's family history, into her suitor's lives—their failed marriages, financial disasters, struggles with confidence men-- and into Harry's eccentric business. We discover how layered seduction as espionage can be; and

how the future in reverse requires an additional narrator. The novel allows the viewer to re-enter the stream from a different place. The immerse journey of the data narrative becomes an aquifer underneath, like two media sharing the same time-based platform. Of course, all novels leaves excisions, spaces between in yet another way. Indeed this is what, since the 1980s, interactive fiction has promised to be.

The four essays of the book serve as another layer of contrapuntal meaning. Readers and viewers make the transit from text to image, and back again—from narrative hooks in the story, to the spaces between fiction and non-fiction, collective memory and incomplete versions of the modern. The essays show how the act of writing history bears some similarity to the pleasures of constructing interactive databases.

The double object of *The Imaginary 20th Century* combines digital and print storytelling, novel writing and scholarship. Yet each of those things exists as those things. "At once a comic picaresque and a treatise on the last century, the piece is a playful and yet deadly serious meditation on one sentence: the future can only be told in reverse."

NET RESULTS

C. Cole Phillips, *"Net Results" Life* (1911)

상상의 20세기에서의 이중 목적

Norman M. Klein와 Margo Bistis

상상의 *20세기*는 노먼 M. 클라인과 마고 비스트스가 저술한 코믹 역사 소설이며, 미디어 박물관 ZKM를 통해 출판되었다. 아티스트 팀과 함께 저자는 사실과 소설, 역사와 전설이 분열되고 회귀하는 독특한 서사 엔진을 구축하였다. 시청자는 두 세기와 세 대륙에 걸친 등장인물들과 함께 한다.

전설에 따르면 1901년 캐리라는 젊은 여성이 유럽을 여행하며 다가오는 세기에 대한 각기 다른 버전인 네 명의 남자에게 구애를 받는다. 필연적으로, 미래는 선택에 따라 달라진다. 우리는 캐리의 불운과 그와 그의 연인이 알아차리지 못한 것들을 보며 캐리 연인의 삶을 따라간다. 글을 읽을수록 캐리의 삶이 삼촌의 사업과 정치 공작에 연루되었음을 알게 된다. 40년 이상 해리 브라운은 과두 정치가들에 의해 고용되어 그들의 범죄를 지우는 역할을 해왔다. 따라서 그가 종종 설명하는 것처럼 간첩 활동은 유혹의 한 형태이다.

해리는 일종의 잠겨 있는 상자이다. 그의 고객은 그가 어떤 것이든 묻어 버릴 수 있다고 생각했고, 그는 최소 법적으로 이를 보장했다. 그의 이런 약속은 1908년 캐리가 무정부주의 정치에 깊이 휘말려 뉴욕에서 한 남자를 총으로 쐈을 때 금이 가기 시작했다. 다행히 범죄는 재판으로 넘어가지 않았다. 1917년에는 해리가 조카에 관한 기록을 남기도록 영감을 주는 다른 스캔들이 이어진다. 이는 해리가 그의 조카를 그녀가 (꽤 자주) 없을 때도 대리로 만나는 방법이기도 하다. 해리는 매우 현대적이며 효율적인 것을 좋아했다. 그는 정보나 전자기기를 통해 사람들을 연락망 안에 두었다.

아카이브는 말 그대로 기계에 의해 작동되었다. 트랙 위에 있는 기어가 금속 슬리브의 카드를 따라 밀었다. 수천 개의 문서를 뒤로, 앞으로, 옆으로 굴릴 수 있는 이 장치는 조선소에서 지어졌다. 이 장치는 주로 첫 번째는 유혹의 소설, 두 번째는 간첩 활동을 위한 고문서로 동작하였다.

상상의 *20세기*는 2,200개의 희귀 사진과 초기 영화, 해설자의 목소리, 인터렉티브 지도를 포함한 방대한 디지털 아카이브와 시청자가 관람할 수 있는 공간을 동원한다. 설명적 인터페이스의 데이터 서사 (www.imaginary20thcentury.com)는 고고학 발굴과 유사한 상호 작용을 유도한다. 시청자는 챕터 지도에 연결되어 각각의 음악적 파노라마를 가진 겹겹이 쌓여있는 이미지 카드들을 이리저리 움직이고 살펴보며 스토리를 파헤친다. 챕터 지도는 장소에 관한 것이기도 하고 동시에 이야기의

일부로써 심리를 나타내는 마파문디 (중세시대의 세계지도)이기도 하다. 해설자의 목소리는 "캐리의 아카이브" 저자가 남겨두기로 한 정보는 추론의 여지를 남긴 체 흐름상 중요한 단서를 제시한다.

카드 다자인은 제1차 세계 대전 이전의 시대에 인쇄된 카드의 편재성을 가진다. 당시 카드는 사교 수단의 사진 카드와 엽서, 홈 엔터테인먼트가 목적인 입체 카드, 도서관 및 기록 보관소용 카드 카탈로그, 정부를 위한 인구 조사 기계, 그뿐만 아니라 비즈니스 데이터 처리를 위한 필수 도구이기도 했다. 또한, 도표 작성자를 위한 펀치카드는 컴퓨터가 있기 훨씬 전에 존재했다.

이야기의 시점인 1893년부터 1925년까지의 역사적인 연구는 도시, 몸, 산업 및 기술, 제국주의, 전쟁 및 사회 운동을 중심으로 광범위하게 이루어졌다. 이 연구는 스토리 개발과 컬렉션 구축 사이, 저작과 기획 사이를 오가는 과정을 수반한다. "캐리의 아카이브"는 1900년 경의 잡지 일러스트레이션, 만화, 사진, 영화, 산업디자인, 건축 도면, 공상 과학, 판타지 및 유토피아 소설, 의학 서적을 포함한 구매체와 신매체를 아우른다. 아카이브는 시각 매체와 인쇄 매체가 대조적으로 결합되며 데이터 서사로 발전되었다.

1816년에는 이러한 기술과 문화의 대조적 결합에 대한 이름이 지어졌다. 그 해, 독일 철학자 프리드리히 셀링은 이러한 소설을 큰 홀 내부의 물시계처럼 움직이는 소설이라고 표현했다. 프리드리히는 이를 'wunder-roman'이라 불렀다. 전통적으로, wunder-roman은 이야기의 중요한 부분이 빠져있는 경우에만 말이 된다. 잃어버린 조각들은 마키나 (정신적 그림)에 영감을 준다고 한다. 18세기에 마키나로 보통 판화나 움직이는 인형극을 지탱했다. wunder-roman은 종종 비도덕적 질서로 단서를 숨긴다. 이는 악한들의 끝나지 않은 비즈니스다. 해리가 등장하는 부분에서, 그는 50년 후 손상된 이미지로 인해 잘못 기록된 좌우로 흔들리는 비행선과 곤충 헬리콥터 같은 허구에서나 가능했던 실현되지 않는 아이디어들에 집착하게 된다.

상상의 *20세기* 데이터 서사에서 없어진 부분들은 소설과 수필 집필에 큰 영감을 주었다. 사실과 허구를 여는 별개의 요소인 책은 독립적이지만 충분한 이야기 전달을 위해 필수적이다. 저자는 해리가 남기기로 한 정보에 더 이상 의존하지 않는다. 해리의 시각 너머를 조사하면서, 소설은 해리가 의도적으로 기록하지 않은 캐리의 세계에 대한 단서를 제공한다. 독자들은 캐리의 가족사부터 그녀의 구혼자의 삶에 대해 알게 되며 실패한 결혼생활, 재정 파탄, 신용 사기꾼들과의 마찰, 그리고 해리의

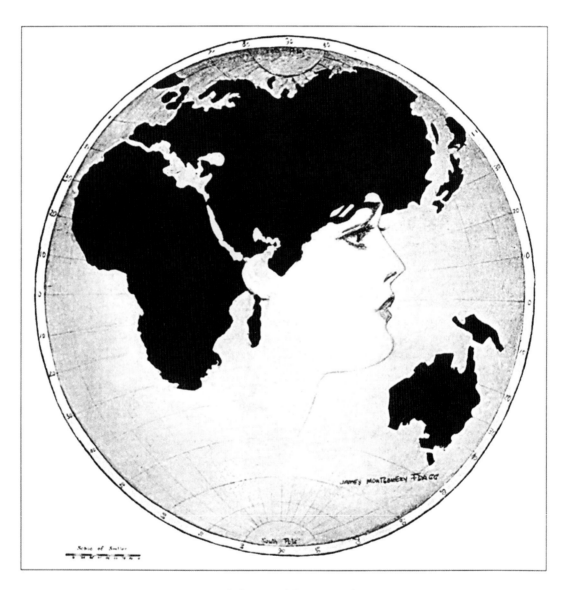

"A Map of the World as Seen by Him"

James Montgomery Flagg, *"The World as Seen by Him,"* Life (1905)

별난 사업에 대해서도 알게 된다. 우리는 유혹이 간첩과 같이 얼마나 복잡해질 수 있는지, 그리고 다른 결과의 미래가 어떻게 부가적인 설명을 필요로 하게 되는지 발견하게 된다. 이 소설에서 독자는 서사의 다른 시점에 다시 들어갈 수 있다.

데이터 나래이티브의 몰입형 여정은 같은 플랫폼을 공유하는 두 매체와 같이 스토리의 근간이 된다. 물론 각각의 소설은 진행이 됨에 따라 분리되어 다른 길로 흐르지만 말이다. 이는 실제로 1980년대 인터렉티브 소설의 흔한 형식이기도 하다.

이 책에 수록된 네 편의 에세이는 각각 대조적인 의미의 겹들을 형성한다. 독자는 글에서 이미지로, 이야기 서사에서 사실과 허구 사이, 집단기억과 불완전한 현대에 대한 기록 사이를 오간다. 이 글은 역사를 기술하는 행위가 대화형의 데이터베이스를 구축하는 즐거움과 어떻게 유사한지 보여준다.

*상상의 20세기*의 이중 목적은 디지털 및 인쇄물의 스토리텔링, 소설 작문 및 학문을 결합한 것이다. 그러나 각각의 목적은 그들 고유의 목적으로써 존재한다. "지난 세기 코믹 악당 소설이자 논문이었던 이 작품은 장난스럽지만, '미래는 오로지 반대로 말해진다'는 말에 대한 진지한 명상이다.

Norman M. Klein is a novelist, media and urban historian. He is the author of the award-winning media novel *Bleeding Through: Layers of Los Angeles, 1920-1986* (a co-production of ZKM/Center for Art & Media Karlsruhe and The Labyrinth Project/USC, 2003). His other works include *The History of Forgetting: Los Angeles* and the Erasure of Memory; *7 Minutes: The Life and Death of the American Animated Cartoon*; *The Vatican to Vegas: The History of Special Effects*; *Freud in Coney Island and Other Tales.* He is on faculty of the School of Critical Studies at California Institute of the Arts.

Norman M. Klein은 소설가이자 미디어 및 도시사학자이다. 그는 수상 경력이 있는 미디어 소설 Bleeding Through: Layers of Los Angeles, 1920-1986 (ZKM 박물관/ 예술 및 미디어 센터 카를스루 미로 프로젝트/ USC, 2003 협업)의 공동저자다. 그의 다른 작품으로는 잊어버린 역사: 로스엔젤레스와 기억의 소멸 (The History of Forgetting: Lost Angeles and the Erasure of Memory) 및 7분: 미국 애니메이션 만화의 삶과 죽음 (7 Minutes: The Life and Death of the American Animated Cartoon), 바티칸에서 베가스로: 특수효과의 역사 (The Vatican to Vegas: The History of Special Effects), 프로이트가 코니아일랜드에서 (Freud in Coney Island and Other Tales)가 있다. California Institute of the Arts 의 비평학과 교수로 재직 중이다.

Margo Bistis는 문화사학자이자 독립적인 큐레이터다. 그녀의 큐레이터 프로젝트에는 2003년 Getty Reasearch Institute)가 주최한 "만화예술: 파리풍의 커리커처"가 있다. 그녀의 출판물은 철학적 현대주의와 풍자만화 및 도시문화에 대한 학술 저널 에세이가 포함된다. 현재 Art Center Collage of Design의 인문과학부 교수로 재직 중이다.

Margo Bistis is a cultural historian and an independent curator. Her curatorial projects include "Comic Art: The Paris Salon in Caricature," organized by the Getty Research Institute in 2003. Her publications include essays in scholarly journals on philosophical modernism, caricature, and urban culture. She is on the faculty of the Humanities & Sciences Department at Art Center College of Design.

ALYONA LARIONOVA

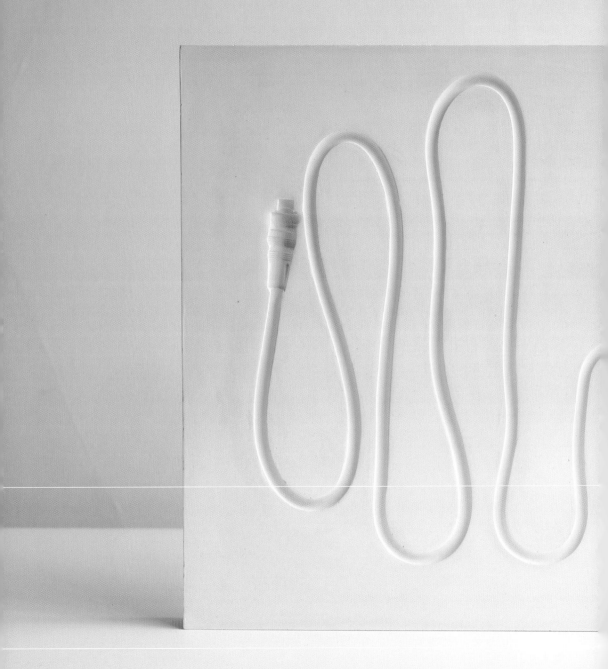

Deciphering codes pertaining to the question of what is happening to us right now is at the heart of this work. At present, all of the data and information we collect can be interpreted only to a certain point, nevertheless the aim is to compute, predict, influence, control and even prevent future behaviours, acting under the economic and security pretext. These statistical and cold interpretations based on data and algorithms pretend to be objective and true, denying a possibility of any subjective interpretation from a personal and critical position, from within and simultaneously from outside the system. Pairing up free jazz with vastness of big data, *Across Lips* attempts to decode the meaning of telling a story in a digital age. Set against the gradual and comprehensive expansion of the Internet Archive, this film redefines what it means to believe in something.

지금 우리에게 일어나고 있는 일에 대한 질문에 대한 암호를 해독하는 것이 이 작업의 핵심이다. 현재, 수집하는 모든 데이터와 정보는 목표는 어떤 시점에서만 해석 가능하며, 그럼에도 불구하고 이는 계산, 예측, 영향, 통제 그리고 나아가 미래의 행동을 제어하거나 심지어 차단하는 행위, 경제적, 안보 개입을 목적으로 한다. 데이터와 알고리즘을 기반으로 한 이런 통계적 냉정한 해석은 객관적이고 사실인 것처럼 가장하며 이 시스템 내외적으로는 개인적이고 비평적인 입장의 모든 주체적 해석의 가능성을 부인한다. 프리 재즈와 대용량 데이터의 방대함을 병치하며, 작품 *입술 너머*는 디지털 시대의 서사가 가지는 의미에 대한 해독을 시도한다. 인터넷 아카이브의 점진적이고 포괄적인 확장에 대비하여, 이 영화는 무언가를 믿는 것이 의미하는 바를 재정의한다.

Alyona Larionova, *Moving Together, Like a Flock of Birds* (2014), plaster

Alyona Larionova (b. 1988, Moscow) earned her BA in Photography from London College of Communications in 2010 and her MFA from Slade School of Fine Art, UCL in 2013. Her works have been exhibited internationally at HOW Art Museum in Wenzhou, National Centre for Contemporary Arts in Moscow, Temnikova & Kasela in Tallinn and Bermodsey Project Space in London. Additionally, the artist's latest film was widely screened at film and video festivals, including Les Rencontres Internationales Paris/Berlin, Open Film 2016, invited by Ed Atkins and Outpost Norwich, as well as Aural Aesthetics Program of the Flatpack Film Festival in Birmingham, among others.

Alyona Larionova는 2010년 London College of Communications에서 미술 학사를 취득한 후 2013년 Slade School of Fine Art, UCL에서 미술 석사 학위를 취득했다. 그녀의 작업물은 원저우의 HOW Art Museum, 모스크바의 National Centre for Contemporary Arts, 런던 Tallinn & Bermodsey 갤러리의 프로젝트 스페이스 등에서 국제적으로 전시되었다. 또한, 작가의 가장 최신 영화는 프랑스/베를린 Les Rencontres Internationales, Ed Atkins, Open Film 2016, 버밍험의 Aural Aesthetics Program of the Flatpack Film Festival 등과 같은 영화 및 영상제에서 상영되었다.

GILI LAVY

Gili Lavy, *Shades* (2016), still from digital video

Gili Lavy's works are predominantly in the medium of sculptural installations and Moving Image, taking the form of various executions, large-scale projections and installation work. Her practice is predicated upon the investigation of social anthropology and collective histories, through belief structure analysis. She focus on the shifting borders between conventional faith and her own constructed beliefs systems, in order to shift perspectives, alter rituals, and question contemporary perception on classical structures. Lavy's work is making a use of traditional sacraments, by their historical origins, and shifting it into its contemporary alternative. Lavy constructs belief systems and their accounts, inspired by existing faiths and sites, whose histories reveal and obstruct the present. With each piece she construct a singular account, as a means upon reflecting a greater collective history and our personal and cultural identities. Through creating journeys of fragments of time, silent sites, and unknown monuments, she attempt to reassemble an experience lived out of order, floating through different states of mind.

Lavy's work looks at subverting our knowledge of truth and faith, through historical and contemporary analysis, in order to raise questions and reflect on our own cultural and social identity.

Gili Lavy은 주로 조각 설치와 다양한 방식으로 설치된 영상, 대규모 프로젝션 및 설치 작업을 한다. 그녀의 작품은 신념 구조 분석을 통한 사회 인류학, 집단적 역사에 대한 연구를 근간으로 한다. Lavy는 관점을 바꾸고, 의례를 개혁하며, 전통적 구조에 현대적 관점에 의문을 제기하기 위해 보편적 신념과 그녀만의 구축된 신념 체계 간의 경계를 재구축하고자 한다. 그녀는 역사적인 기원을 따라 진행된 전통적 성찬식을 현 대에 맞게 변형하는 작업을 하였다. Lavy는 현재를 드러내며 가로막은 기존의 신앙과 장소에서 영감을 받아 신념 체계와 해석을 구축한다. 작품을 통해 그녀는 더 큰 집단역사와 개인적 문화적 정체성을 반영하는 각각의 해석을 만든다. 시간의 파편과 은밀한 장소, 무명의 기념비를 만드는 여정을 통해 그녀는 서로 다른 상태의 마음을 거치는 삶의 경험을 재현하고자 한다.

Lavy는 작품에서 우리 자신의 문화적 사회적 정체성에 의문을 던지고, 이를 반영하기 위해 역사적인 그리고 현대적 분석을 하고, 진리와 신앙을 재정립하고자 한다.

Gili Lavy, *Shades* (2016), still from digital video

Gili Lavy, (1987. Israel) London based artist works across sculptural installations and large-scale video projections. Lavy received her Master degree from the Royal College of Art, London UK. During 2017 Lavy was invited to exhibit her work in the CICA Museum, South Korea and awarded a finalist for the Mario Merz Prize 2nd edition in Italy. During 2016 Lay was invited to show her work in the Whitechapel Gallery London, CAFA Art Museum Beijing, and Art Basel Switzerland. During the same year Lavy was awarded the The Clore Duffield foundation Grant for exceptional talent. Solo shows contain Fieldworks Gallery London UK, Jerusalem Artist House Israel and Hongik Museum Seoul South Korea. Her work has been exhibited widely including Belo Horizonte's International Biennale of Photography in Brazil, Art Basel, Tel Aviv Museum of Art, Prix Europa Berlin, Off Print Tate Modern, Art Dubai, Lo Schermo Dell'arte Florence, Unit London, Centre for Contemporary Art TLV, New Now Amsterdam to name a few. Lavy's work investigates the shifting borders between conventional faiths and her own constructed beliefs systems. Her work reflects upon the transitions within several beliefs, and their implication on existence. These transitioning realities, within lands, forgotten histories and theological views, are examined by Lavy's own superimposed belief system. She has been awarded and nominated for Awards including; Bloomberg New Contemporaries London, Blooom Award by Warsteiner Germany, Visio Young Acquisition Prize Florence, HIX award and Spectrum Artists Moving Image, London, England Arts Council to name a few. Her work is represented in both public and private international collections.

Gili Lavy는 런던에 기반을 둔 작가로 조각 설치 및 대규모 비디오 프로젝션 작업을 한다. 영국 런던의 Royal College of Art에서 석사 학위를 받았다. 2017년에 Lavy는 CICA 미술관 (한국)으로부터 작품 전시 초청을 받았고, Mario Merz Prize (이탈리아)에서 최종 후보로 수여됐다. 2016년에는 Whitechapel Gallery London과 CAFA Art Museum Beijing, Art Basel Switzerland에 초청되어 작품을 선보였다. 같은 해, The Clore Duffield Foundation 재단으로부터 재능을 인정받아 보조금을 수여 받았다. 영국 Fieldworks Gallery London과 이스라엘 Jerusalem Artist House, 국내 홍익미술관에서 개인전 경험이 있다. 이외에도 브라질 Belo Horizonte's International Biennale of Photograph, Art Basel, Tel Aviv Museum of Art, Prix Europa Berlin, Off Print Tate Modern, Art Dubai, Lo Schermo Dell'arte Florence, Unit London, Centre for Contemporary Art TLV, New Now Amsterdam 등 많은 곳에서 전시되었다. Lavy는 전통적인 믿음과 그녀 자신의 신념 체계 사이의 긴장감 및 변화를 연구한다. 그녀의 작품은 여러 신념 내의 변화와 존재에 대한 암시를 투영한다. 변화하는 현실, 영토, 잊혀진 과거와 이론들은 Lavy 만의 함축적 신념 체계에 의해 해석된다. 그녀는 Bloomberg New Contemporaries London, Warsteiner Germany의 Bloom Award, Visio Young Acquisition Prize Florence, HIX, 또한 London, England Arts Council의 Specturem Artists Moving Image 등 많은 곳에서 수상 및 수상 후보로 지명되었다. 그녀의 작업물은 공공 및 사설 국제 컬렉션으로 소장되어 있다.

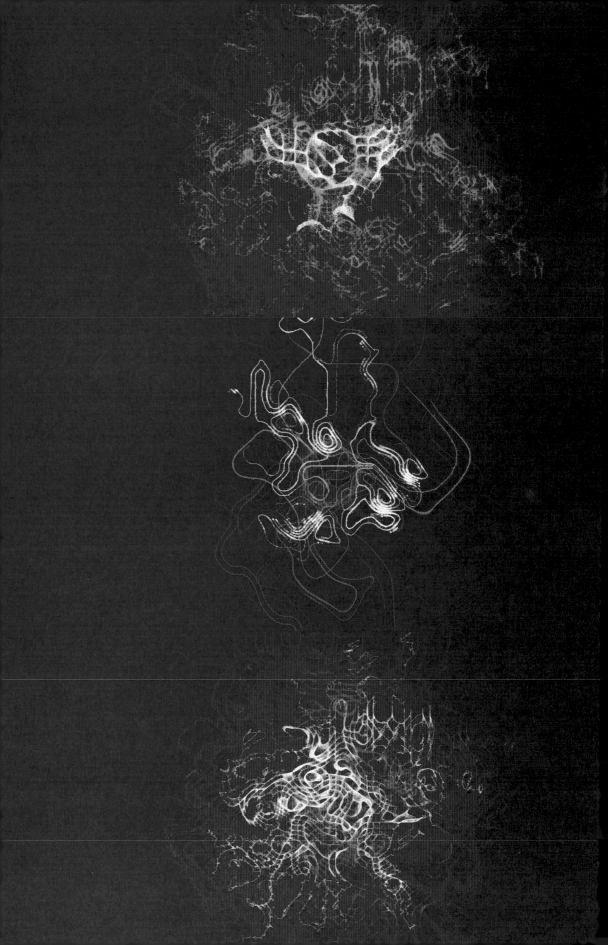

WAYNE MADSEN

Perlin noise is a form of randomly generated values in a computer that look more organic than traditional random seed values. Referred to a procedurally generated', the random values build on previously assigned computations. This approach has been used in computer graphics to do things like automatically creating natural looking landscapes in video games. This html5 canvas project unfolds based on a number of external variables, including screen resolution, to create a unique time-based visual each time the piece is visited. I see myself as curator of the art generated by computer algorithms. The computer art I create uses generative algorithms and small, random variations to develop unique views each time the work is visited; I Have written the system, but it is the computing device which applies its own 'creativity' into the creation of what is seen. It is amazing to me that altering just a few key variables can have drastic affects visually, just as people are connected but infinitely varied. There is beauty in these small differences, these small moments, these defining characteristics.

펄린 노이즈는 컴퓨터에서 무작위로 생성된 값의 형태로 이전의 무작위 시드 값보다 더 유기적으로 보인다. '절차적으로 생성된' 무작위 값은 이전에 할당 된 계산을 기반으로 한다. 이 접근법은 비디오 게임에서 자연스럽게 보이는 풍경을 자동으로 만드는 것과 같은 일을 하기 위해 컴퓨터 그래픽에 사용되었다. 이 html5 캔버스 프로젝트는 화면 해상도를 비롯한 다양한 외부 변수를 기반으로 전개되어 작품을 접할 때마다 독특한 영상을 생성한다. 나는 나 자신을 컴퓨터 알고리즘에 의해 생성된 예술을 선정하는 큐레이터로 여긴다. 내가 만든 컴퓨터 아트는 생성 알고리즘과 작고 무작위적인 변형을 사용하여 작품을 접할 때마다 독특한 모습으로 변모한다. 나는 이 시스템을 만들었지만, 결과물의 탄생에 자신의 '창의력'을 적용하는 것은 컴퓨팅 장치이다. 사람들이 연결되어 있지만 무한히 다양하듯이, 몇 가지 변수를 변경해 전혀 다른 영상을 만들어낼 수 있다는 것은 놀라운 일이다. 이러한 작은 차이, 작은 순간, 결정적인 특징에 아름다움이 있다.

Wayne Madsen, *Bloom* (2016), html canvas and javascript

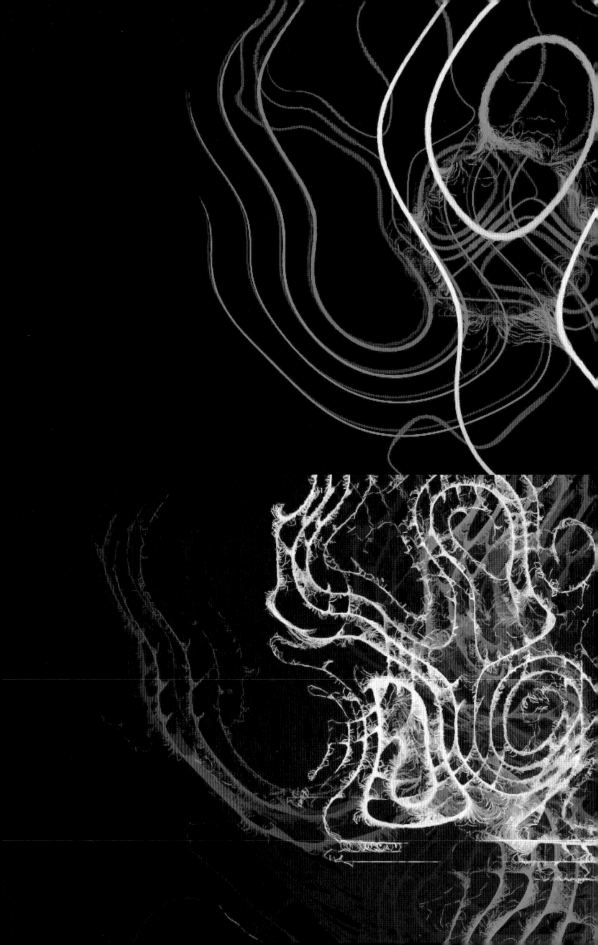

Wayne Madsen is a new media artist and educator specializing in algorithmic practices and human computer interactions. He earned his MFA at the CADRE New Media laboratory, where he participated in exhibiting at and organizing the Zero1 International Art Festival. Wayne has taught digital art at Bowling Green State University and Dakota State University focusing in virtual environments and physical computing. He currently teaches new media and web design at Indiana University, Kokomo and resides in Indiana, USA

Wayne Madsen은 뉴 미디어 아티스트이자 교육자로 알고리즘 실습과 사람과 컴퓨터 간의 상호 작용을 연구한다. 그는 CAD-RE New Media laboratory에서 미술 석사를 취득했고, 제로 1 국제 예술제의 전시 및 조직에 참여했다. Wayne은 버울링 그린 주립 대학에서 디지털 아트를, 다코타 주립 대학에서 가상 현실과 물리적 컴퓨팅을 가르쳤다. 그는 현재 코코모 인디에나 대학에서 뉴 미디어와 웹 디자인을 가르치고 있으며 미국 인디에나에 거주하고 있다.

Wayne Madsen, *Bloom* (2016), html canvas and javascript

KUSHTRIM MEHMETI

"Man on Cross-book"
November 5, 2016
Facebook as the biggest social network, it became an inseparable part of our lives. Spending time and emotional connections with this social network is getting a big problem for us.
Man on Cross-book symbolizes the crucified humans with the social network that exhausts our time.
©Kushtrim Mehmeti
Photo : Qëndresa Jashari

"Unsecured paper"
August 30, 2016
A beggar, but not like everyone else, a graduate who can't work in his professional field. We can see the poverty on his legs and sadness on his face.
©Kushtrim Mehmeti
Photo : Ylli Tahiraj

"Reality"
October 15, 2016
A powerful man leads people who don't think but just walk like sheep. Lies, different treatments by the leaders, and ways of accepting things from people are just somethings that are showed on this photography.
©Kushtrim Mehmeti
Photo : Vlora Dajaku

"십자가-북 위의 사람"
2016년 11월 5일
가장 큰 SNS로 성장한 페이스북은 우리의 삶에서 떼려야 뗄 수 없는 일부가 되었다. 시간과 감정적 유대를 이 SNS에 소비하는 것은 우리에게 큰 문제가 되고 있다.
십자가북 위의 사람은 소셜 네트워크에 시간을 못 박는 사람들을 상징한다.
©쿠쉬트림 메흐메디
사진 : Qëndresa Jashar

"보장 없는 종이쪼가리"
2016년 8월 30일
구걸하는 거지이지만 다른 이들과는 달리 그는 학력은 있지만, 그 전공을 살릴 수 없는 남자이다. 그의 다리에서 가난을, 얼굴에서 슬픔을 읽을 수 있다.
©쿠쉬트림 메흐메디
사진 : Gëzim Hasani

"현실"
2016년 10월 15일
한 강인한 남자가 사람들을 이끌고, 대중들은 생각 없는 양처럼 걷는다. 이 작품은 거짓말들, 지도자 다른 처방들, 사람들로부터 받아들이는 방법들을 표현하였다.
©쿠쉬트림 메흐메디
사진 : Vlora Dajaku

Kushtrim Mehmeti, *Unsecured paper* (2016), (top)
Kushtrim Mehmeti, *Techonology* (2016), (middle)
Kushtrim Mehmeti, *Reality* (2016), (bottom)

Kushtrim Mehmeti, *Death of Kosovo* (2016), (top)
Kushtrim Mehmeti, *Hope Die Last* (2016), (bottom)

"Death of Kosovo"
February 26, 2017
After 9 years as an independent country, Kosovo still walks in the wrong direction involving organized crime, corruption and lack of freedom of expression.
The work depicts a crime scene surrounded with strips that suggests not to cross. A map of Kosovo shows her own death, a number of evidences show us factors that brought "Kosovo death:" 1.Coruption, 2.Organized crime, 3.Politicians, 4.Health, and 5.Education.
©Kushtrim Mehmeti
Photo&Drawing : Dardan Rushiti

"Hope Dies Last "
Octemter 29, 2016
The government would kill anyone who hampers them, shut those few opportunities that people have and they kill openly or secretly.
The desert show us the miserable situation that we are in. The man with a sword symbolizes the power of government, and the last prisoner waiting to be executed is hope. Tired, on the eve of death but still with hope.
©Kushtrim Mehmeti
Photo : Gëzim Hasani

Kushtrim Mehmeti was born in Kosovo on 16.01.1988. In his early teens he developed an interest in directing, in 2011 he was accepted at the Academy of fine Arts in Pristina. Mehmeti made the next step forward in his career when he was accepted at Faculty of Arts in Kosovo, where he was teached by Prof.Elmaze Nura. , Mehmeti's work in 2011-17; consist of theater plays : "Comedy of Errors," "Macbeths Fragment", "Waiting for Train," "Twin Clowns," "This property is commended."

Kushtrim Mehmeti는 1988년 1월 16일 코소보에서 태어났다. 십 대 시절부터 그는 연출에 흥미를 느꼈다. 2011년 Mehmeti는 프리슈티나의 the Academy of fine Arts 에 입학한다. Elmaze Nura 교수가 있는 코소보의 Faculty of Arts에 입학했을 때 Mehmeti는 자신의 경력이 한 단계 발전할 수 있을 거란 기대를 하게 된다. 2011년부터 2017년까지 작품 "Comedy of Errors," "Macbeths Fragment," "Waiting for Train," "Twin Clowns," "This property is commended"의 연극 공연을 하였다.

"코소보의 죽음"
2017년 4월 26일
독립된 국가가 된 지 9년 후, 코소보는 여전히 잘못된 방향으로 가고 있다. 조직된 범죄와 부패, 표현의 자유가 우리를 방해하는 이유다.
작품에서 범죄 현장으로 넘어가는 것을 금지하는 선으로 둘러싸여 있다. 코소보 지도는 국토의 죽음을 보여주며, "코소보의 죽음"을 가져 수많은 원인을 보여준다. 1. 부정부패, 2. 조직범죄, 3. 정치인들, 4. 의료, 그리고 5. 교육.

"희망이 마지막으로 죽는다"
2016년 10월 29일
코소보 정부는 그들을 방해하는 모두를 죽이고, 민중이 가진 작은 가능성 조차 닫아 버리고 공개적, 비공개적으로 죽인다.
사진 속 사막은 우리가 처한 비참한 상황을 보여준다. 검을 지닌 남자는 정부의 권력을, 마지막 처형을 기다리는 사형수는 "희망"이다. 죽음의 문전에서 지쳤지만, 여전히 희망을 품고.
©쿠쉬트림 메흐메디
사진 : Gëzim Hasani

TRACY MILLER-ROBBINS

Strange Neighbours:

Between the Personal and the Interpersonal in Tracy Miller-Robbins Animation Installation

by Aaron J. Petten

With her sketchbook like approach to imagery, Tracy Miller-Robbins' animated installation, *Strange Neighbours* (USA, 2016-7), resonates with expressionistic complexity and nuance that transcends the simplicity of her visual style. Her style is reminiscent of a tradition of animation shaped by the likes of the Zagreb School and the National Film Board of Canada. But her gallery installation format and approach to exhibition is more reminiscent of the audiovisual art of Neo-Dada and Pop Art.

Strange Neighbours is a piece that is stark in its tones, both visually and conceptually. Her formal approach coincides with the multiplanar cartoons of Dutch animator, Paul Driessen. But her scale and mode of exhibition more closely parallels the audiovisual installation work of Fluxus and Neo-Dada art. The piece is a projection of a recurring loop of animation separated between fourteen separate panels across six rows resembling comic strip or comic book panels, which are thematically rather than narratively linked — the imagery both contrastive and complementary. Miller-Robbins uses extremely muted tones — greenish and bluish greys, black, and white negative space — which ultimately appears as an enhanced grey scale. Through her limited color scheme, she conveys a plethora of imagery that is both semi-figurative and semi-abstract. From top to bottom, the first and fourth row are image facsimiles with offset animated timing. Some panels show three separate sequence loops of hidden figures that approximates Munch's figure from The Scream. While other panels convey disembodied watching eyes in darkness that are peeping behind blinds in anxious anticipation. The second and fifth row includes two outreaching arms coming from both the left and right of the projected surface engaging in a handshake that release and recede to the edges of the screen before disappearing and cycling

through again. The third and sixth rows include two silhouetted faces that metamorphose from human to animal correspond with the shifting emotional state of the figures, which transform from rage to affection and love before cycling through anew. The imagery conjuring a likeness to Chinese shadow puppetry and the silhouette animation of Lotte Reiniger.

The recurring and patterned quality of *Strange Neighbours* emanates qualities that resemble interior design techniques, which results in the transcendence of the piece's installation format as being a fixture not unlike ornamental textile designs. Yet the piece is far from ornamental decorum. The projected mode of presentation invokes associations with video projection mapping while the recurring looping quality of the piece invokes associations with the cyclical low-fi property of gifs. Conceptually echoing the likes of fellow experimental animator, Jan Švankmajer's Dimensions of Dialogue (1982), Miller-Robbins seems to be addressing the status of interpersonal communication and interaction. Švankmajer broached various facets of communication through the surrealist grotesque by using an array of materials and stop-motion. However, Miller-Robbins' work is stylistically more indicative of the great modern poetic animators such as Caroline Leaf and Don Hertzfeldt. Her sketchy, draftswoman-like style retains the residue of the illustrative process, which feeds into the poetry that she creates through her panels. *Strange Neighbours* adroitly addresses the vulnerabilities and anxieties surrounding communication or a lack thereof. Whether this is indicative of a broader social observation or point being made by the artist, a personalization of the artist's own hesitancy and insecurities with interpersonal interactions and communication, or a combination of the two remains ambiguous.

The installation format, on a constant loop, reiterates and reinforces the communicational dimensions of the piece and the constant anxieties that resurface with each encounter. In this way, the form itself enhances if not carries as much meaning as the motifs of the content itself.

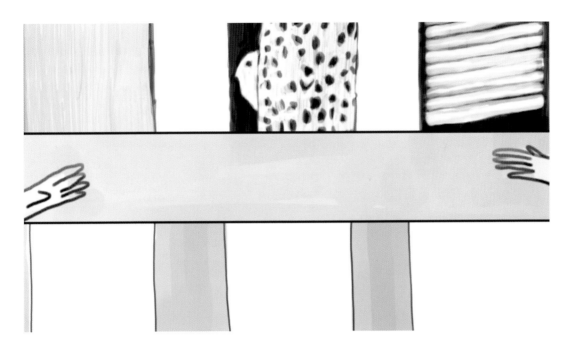

Tracy Miller Robbins, *Strange Neighbours Single Channel* (2015) (top)
Tracy Miller Robbins, *Strange Neighbours Museum of Contemporary Art Media Facade Three Channel* (2014) (bottom)

Tracy Miller Robbins, *Strange Neighbours Original Sketch (2014)*

수상한 이웃:

개인과 인간관계 사이, Trracy Miller-Robbins 설치 애니메이션

Aaron J. Petten

트레이시의 드로잉 같은 영상 설치물 수상한 *이웃* (미국, 2016-17)은 시각적 스타일의 단순함을 초월해 표현적 복잡성과 뉘앙스를 지닌다. 그녀의 스타일은 자그레브 학교와 캐나다 국립 영화 위원회가 추구하는 애니메이션의 전통을 연상케 한다. 그러나 그녀의 전시 공간에서의 작품 설치 방식은 네오다다와 팝 아트의 시청각 예술과 관련이 깊어 보인다.

수상한 *이웃*은 시각적으로나 개념적으로나 삭막한 작품이다. 그녀의 접근 방식은 네덜란드 애니메이터 Paul Driessen의 멀티플래너 만화와 비슷하다. 그러나 작품의 규모와 방식은 플럭서스와 네오다다 시청각 설치 작업물과 더 유사하다. 이 작품은 반복 재생되는 애니메이션 루프를 이용한 전시로, 6 개의 반복적인 만화책 조각이나 만화책 표지를 가로지르는 14 개의 별도 패널로 이루어져 있으며, 각각의 영상은 스토리보다는 주제적으로 반대나 보완적 관계로 연결되어 있다. Miller-Robbins 는 푸르스름한 회색이나 흑백의 극단적인 모노톤을 사용한다. 그녀는 제한적 색상으로 수많은 반구상과 반추상 이미지를 조합한다. 위에서 아래로, 첫 번째와 네 번째 줄은 복제된 이미지들이 상쇄되며 병치된다. 일부 패널은 뭉크의 절규와 비슷한 숨겨진 형태의 세 가지 반복 애니메이션을 보여준다. 한편 어떤 패널에서는 블라인드 뒤의 어둠 속에서 엿보고 있는 알 수 없는 눈이 보인다. 두 번째 줄과 다섯 번째 줄에는 두 팔이 화면의 왼쪽과 오른쪽에서 나타나 서로 악수를 하고 각자 화면의 가장자리로 물러나 사라지기를 반복한다. 세 번째와 여섯 번째 줄에는 감정 상태가 변화하면서 인간에서 동물로 변형되는 두 개의 얼굴이 있다. 이 얼굴은 분노에서 애정과 사랑으로 변화하며 끝없이 반복된다. 영상은 중국 그림자 인형극과 영화 Lotte Reiniger (실루엣 애니메이션 기법의 개척자)의 실루엣 애니메이션을 연상케 한다.

수상한 *이웃*의 반복적이고 패턴화된 특징은 인테리어 디자인과도 유사하며, 섬유 디자인의 장식적 효과를 준다. 물론 이 작품은 기존 장식적 형태와는 전혀 다르다. 그러나 조각은 장식적인 데코럼에서 멀리 떨어져 있다. 영상이 큰 벽에 비추어졌을 때 비디오 프로젝션 매핑 처럼 보이지만 아이러니하게도 작품의 루프 애니메이션 조각들은 인터넷의 저화질 GIF 애니메이션을 연상케 한다. 실험 애니메이터 Jan Švankmajer의 *대화의 차원* (*Dimensions of Dialogue*, 1982)처럼 Miller-Robbins는 대인 관계에서의 소통에 관해 말하고자 하는 것 같다. Švankmajer는 다양한 매체와 스톱 모션 방식의 초현실주의 그로테스크 양식을 통해 소통의 여러 가지 면을 다루었다. 반면 Miller-Robbins의 작업은 Caroline Leaf와 Don Hertzfeldt와 같은 현대의 시적인 애니메이터들과 스타일 면에서 더 관련이 있어 보인다. 그녀의 손맛이 느껴지는 드로잉 스타일은 여러 개의 패널과 만나며 시적인 느낌을 살려준다. 수상한 *이웃*은 능숙하게 의사소통과 그것의 부재로 인한 나약함과 불안한 감정들을 보여준다. 이것이 사회적 관찰의 결과물인지, 아니면 작가의 대인 관계에서 겪은 개인적인 주저와 불안한 감정을 표현한 것인지, 아니면 이 두 가지 모두가 혼합된 것인지는 알 수 없다.

이 작품의 설치 버전은 반복되며 실제로 반복되고 있는 의사소통의 문제와 지속적 불안감을 극대화한다. 이 같은 방식으로 본연의 의도나 의미를 떠나 본 작품의 형태와 형식 자체만으로 자신을 스스로 강화해 나가는 것이다.

Tracy Miller-Robbins creates animated drawings about interpersonal experiences. Influenced by Ben Shahn and Caroline Leaf, the works strive to capture this essence, both through gestural marks and figurative gesture. The expression and limited palettes of her work results in pointed thematic motifs that are embedded in seemingly abstract forms. The works, which merge the practices of sketching and animation, have been nationally and internationally presented in festivals and galleries.

Tracy Miller-Robbins는 대인관계에 대한 애니메이션을 만든다. Ben Shahn 과 Caroline Leaf의 영향을 받은 그의 작업은 비언어적 제스처와 몸짓을 통해 이를 표현하고자 한다. 제스처들과 제한된 색상으로 그녀는 추상적 형태에 내재한 주제를 표현한다. 스케치와 애니메이션이 혼합된 그녀의 작품은 국내 및 국제적으로 페스티벌 및 갤러리에서 상영됐다.

JOHN MUTTER

John Mutter, *My Aunts*

John Mutter, *My Dad 01*

John Mutter, *My Dad 03* (top), *Jo Passed 03* (bottom)

John Mutter has blue eyes and a slightly large nose. His hair used to swoosh to the left but now it generally swooshes to the right (from your point of view.) He takes pictures and video with a camera and makes music with instruments and also his computer. Do you like music? Me too. He has a website which probably has music and photos and videos on it. He likes animals and does not choose between dogs or cats. Why would you only choose one? What is wrong with you? His favourite food is probably sushi and maybe curry. Pizza is cool but he developed a wheat allergy a few years ago so now he can't eat regular pizza anymore. Honestly he doesn't miss eating wheat that much. Did you know wheat is usually listed before soy in soy sauce ingredients? Shouldn't it be called wheat sauce? What if we all started referring to it as wheat sauce? John likes to grow vegetables and other plants. He has the ability to speak with animals and can turn invisible. His photographic work focuses on aspects of photography that are often avoided. He chooses images where the models are blinking to use as finals and uses makeup and Photoshop to make them less attractive. K i gotta go so I will ttyl okay?"

John Mutter는 푸른 눈과 약간 큰 코를 가졌다. 예전에는 그의 머리가 약간 왼쪽으로 휘어져 있었는데 현재는 오른쪽으로 휘어 있다 (당신이 보는 관점에서). 그는 카메라로 사진을 찍고 비디오를 촬영하며 악기와 컴퓨터로 음악을 만든다. 당신은 음악을 좋아하는가? 나도 그렇다. 그의 홈페이지에서 그의 음악과 사진, 영상 작품을 감상할 수 있다. 그는 동물을 좋아하지만, 개와 고양이 중 뭐가 더 나은지 고민하지는 않는다. 왜 꼭 둘 중 하나를 골라야 하나? 그런 질문은 왜 하는지 모르겠다. 그가 가장 좋아하는 음식은 아마도 초밥과 카레일 것이다. 피자도 좋지만, 몇 년 전에 밀가루 알레르기가 발견되어서 이제 일반적인 피자는 먹지 못한다. 솔직히 밀가루 음식을 못 먹는다는 것이 그렇게 아쉽지만은 않다. 당신은 간장 소스에 밀가루가 콩보다 더 많이 들어가는 걸 알고 있는가? 그렇다면 그걸 Soy Sauce (콩 소스: 간장)이 아니라 밀가루 소스라고 불러야 하는 게 아닌가? 우리가 모두 그것을 밀가루 소스라고 부르기 시작하면 어떨지? John은 채소나 식물을 기르는 걸 좋아한다. 그는 동물과 말할 수 있고, 투명 인간이 될 수도 있다. 그의 사진 작업은 일반적으로는 사진에서 피해지는 것들에 대해 다룬다. 그는 모델이 눈을 깜빡이는 순간을 포착하고 덜 매력적이게 보이기 위해 화장을 하거나 포토샵을 이용한다. 여기까지 말하고 다음에 더 얘기해줄게.

VASILIOS PAPAIOANNU

Viscera and the aesthetic world of mental images

Saturated colors unveil our past. Shapes are blurry, lost in layers of thought. In circumscribed landscapes where characters are locked; everything is suspended. The memory of a woman merges with the slow pacing of the camera. Trees become cerebral ramified pathways that connect us with our most sacred emotions. A foreign radio transmission echoes inside our brain, bouncing from wall to wall as if in a stark white room. Two women are playing a peculiar game of silences. Inside that room, time runs out fast, and they are both projected into their common fantasy of death. *Viscera* is a phantasmagorical world containing syncopated stories. The geography of the human body becomes a map to navigate inside the viscera. Fumed sounds surround pieces of forgotten dreams. *Viscera* is a dispersed piece of human subconscious exploded into images.

Vasilios Papaioannu, *Viscera* (2014), still from digital video

When I don't narrate three act stories, I immerse myself in brief cinematic moments. Fast pacing visuals. Stagnant mental images. No succession of events. No human actions. Or maybe syncopated gestures. Colors. Noise. Past. Faces. Parentheses. Everything that is located in between meanings.

Abstractions. Formulaic experimentations. In my work I extend those parentheses. I make them permanent. I transform them into whole worlds where reality is distorted, translated, and abstracted into a new matter. The grainy darkness of reversal film, the superimposed lights, colors, shapes, the errors of digital cinematography. Pixelization. Everything melts into a unified visual extravaganza that interacts with visceral sounds echoing into a new world, a world manufactured by the form. In this world I am happy and serene because I don't have to narrate, I don't have to explain, I don't have to convince. In this world of purity I simply exist, strictly centripetal inside the circumscribed world of the frame.

내장과 심적 이미지의 미학적 세계

완전히 적셔진 색이 우리의 과거를 드러낸다. 모양은 흐릿해지고, 여러 가지 생각 속에 사라진다. 주인공들이 갇힌 닫힌 공간, 모든 것은 정지되어 있다. 여자의 기억은 느린 속도의 카메라와 융합된다. 나무의 형태는 지적인 통로가 되어 우리를 가장 신성한 감정과 연결한다. 외래의 라디오 전파는 메마른 하얀 방 속의 벽에서 벽으로 튀기듯이 우리의 뇌 속에서 메아리친다. 두 여성이 독특한 침묵 게임을 하고 있다. 그 방 안에서 시간은 빠르게 흐르고 둘은 공통된 죽음이란 환상 속으로 투영된다. *내장*은 변칙적 이야기가 담긴 초현실적 세계. 신체 지형은 내장을 탐색할 수 있게 도와주는 지도가 된다. 성난 소리는 잊혀진 꿈의 파편들을 둘러싼다. *내장*에서 인간의 흩어진 잠재의식은 이미지로 폭발한다.

내가 세 가지 이야기를 해설하지 않을 때는 짧은 영화적 순간에 젖어있다. 빠른 속도의 시각 정보들. 침체된 정신적 이미지. 연속적인 사건의 부재, 인간 행동의 부재. 혹은 변칙적 동작들. 색감. 소음. 과거. 얼굴들. 삽입구. 모든 의미 사이에 있는 모든 것들.

추상화. 수식 실험. 내 작품에 이러한 삽입구들을 확장했다. 그들을 영속적으로 만들었다. 나는 이것들을 현실이 왜곡되고, 번역되고, 새로운 문제로 추상화된 완전한 세계로 변화시킨다. 반전 필름의 거친 어두움, 중첩된 조명, 색상, 모양, 디지털 영화의 오류. 픽셀화. 모든 것이 통일된 시각적으로 화려한 볼거리 속에 녹아들었다. 이는 본능적 음향과 함께 형태에 의해 구축된 새로운 세계로 울려 펴진다. 이 세계에서 설명할 필요도, 해명할 필요도, 확신을 줄 필요도 없기 때문에 나는 행복하고 고요하다. 이 순수한 세계에서 난 그저 존재할 뿐이며, 오로지 프레임으로 한정된 세상 속에서만 맴돈다.

Vasilios Papaioannu is a Greek-Italian filmmaker, writer and producer. He holds an MA in Communication/Text Semiotics from the University of Siena and an MFA in Film from Syracuse University. In his work Papaioannu explores the fleeting dreamscapes of reality using noise, movement, and disturbance. In conjunction with his filmmaking activity he is also a mixed media visual artist, combining painting, vector art and photography. He is currently an Assistant Professor at the Department of Transmedia, Film, in the College of Visual and Performing Arts at Syracuse University in New York.

Vasilios Papaioannu는 그리스계 이탈리아인 영화 제작자이자 글작가이며 프로듀서이다. 그는 the University of Siena에서 커뮤니케이션/텍스트 기호학 석사를 이수했고 시러큐스 대학에서 영화학과 박사를 이수했다. 그의 작품에서 Papaioannu는 음향, 움직임 및 소란을 이용해 찰나의 꿈과 같은 현실 풍경을 탐구한다. 영화 제작 활동과 함께 그는 그림, 벡터 아트 및 사진을 결합한 시각 혼합 매체 아티스트다. 그는 현재 뉴욕 시러큐스 대학교 시각, 공연 예술학부에서 트렌스 미디어와 영화과 조교수로 역임하고 있다.

Vasilios Papaioannu, *Viscera* (2014), still from digital video

MIKEY PETERSON

Mikey Peterson, *Slip Away* (2014), still image from digital video

Mikey Peterson's meditative images merge with jolts and jumps via real-time shots and quick-cut edits. Light contrasts through darkened backgrounds, and classical elements—water, fire, air and earth—create abstracted spaces. These distortions, equally influenced by pre-CGI science fiction films, experimental cinema, and sound collage aim to disturb the viewer's self-perception and sense of place. Subtle events appear dramatic and nature's movements become surreal. Footage is manipulated and taken out of their original context in order to relay other truths about the world that it is from. To advance this process of displacement, Peterson manipulates the ambient sound from the source recordings to compose a cohesive soundtrack, moving the viewer into abstract meditations, urban chaos, and dark surreal spaces that paradoxically envelop rhythms of tone and light.

In *Slip Away*, shot on Lake Michigan's shoreline in Chicago, nature distorts of its own accord. It is the combination of water, earth, wind and sun that creates layers of abstract spaces. The scenes are organic, but direction, contrast, speed and sound are manipulated. Through this process, technology and nature work together.

In this one-shot video, buildings hide behind an impressionistic haze, as conflicting symbols of industry and nature seamlessly layer. The imagery is familiar, but it's always at a distance, as movement, light, and sound reinforces its surrealism. The imagery slowly distorts and almost vanishes like memories, which diverge from the experiences they intend to mirror. Memories emerge as an alternate reality we create and revise over time. These visions skew, as our minds focus on fragments of the original experiences - sometimes these visions warp the event to the point where they no longer represent the event but create an alternative version, a dream-like new reality that can influence our present selves. Maybe our selves and our lives are built upon this process of useful mis-remembering. What we see and hear is in constant flux, and the same can be said of what we view as Truth and Self.

Mikey Peterson의 명상적 이미지는 실시간 촬영과 신속한 편집을 통해 충격과 급변함이 더해진다. 어두운 배경을 통해 빛이 대조되고, 고전적인 물과 불, 물, 땅과 같은 요소는 추상적인 공간을 창조한다. CG가 발명되기 전의 공상 과학 영화, 실험 영화 및 사운드 콜라주의 영향을 고르게 받은 이러한 왜곡을 통해 시청자의 자기 인식과 장소감에 불안감을 야기하고자 한다. 미묘한 사건이 극적이 되고 자연의 움직임은 초현실적으로 된다. 세계에 대한 다른 진리를 전달하기 위해 촬영 장면을 조작하고 본래의 문맥을 없앤다. 이러한 의미 변환을 만들기 위해 Peterson은 원본에서 추출한 소리로 배경 음향을 만들고 관객을 추상적인 명상과 도시의 혼돈, 역설적으로 음색과 빛의 리듬이 뒤덮인 어두운 초현실적 공간으로 안내한다.

시카고 미시간 호숫가에서 촬영된 *Slip Away*에서 자연은 자신을 스스로 왜곡한다. 이는 물과 땅, 바람과 태양의 조합은 겹겹의 추상적인 공간을 창조한다. 이 장면들은 자연스러워 보이지만 방향, 명함, 속도와 음향은 조작된 것이다. 이 과정을 통해 기술과 자연은 함께 작동한다.

이 원샷 비디오에서 건물은 인상주의적 안개 속에 가려져 산업과 자연의 충돌하는 상징체계는 부드럽게 겹쳐진다. 이미지는 익숙하지만 움직임과 빛과 소리로 강조되는 초현실주의와 함께 항상 멀리 떨어져 있다.

이미지는 기억과도 같이 본래 재현하고자 했던 경험으로부터 멀어지며 천천히 왜곡되고 거의 사라진다. 우리가 흐르는 시간에 따라 창조하고 재생하는 기억은 우리가 창조하고 지속해서 수정할 수 있는 대체 현실로 떠오른다. 이러한 시각은 우리의 마음이 원래 경험의 파편에 초점을 맞출 때 기억을 새로 각색해내듯 왜곡된다. 이러한 꿈같은 새로운 현실이 된 조작된 기억은 우리의 현 자아에 영향을 줄 수 있다. 어쩌면 우리 자신과 우리의 삶은 이러한 잘못된 기억의 과정에 기반을 두고 있을지 모른다. 우리가 보고 듣는 것은 끝없이 흐르며, 진리와 자아에 대한 우리의 시각 또한 마찬가지로 끝없이 변화한다.

Mikey Peterson is a Chicago-based video-audio artist, singer-songwriter, and art educator. His work has shown at Chicago's Museum of Contemporary Photography; the Chicago Cultural Center; the University of Chicago's Smart Museum; Rome's MAXXI Museum; the Armory Center For The Arts in Pasadena, California; Seattle's Northwest Film Forum; the SIGGRAPH Conference in Los Angeles, California, the Lucca Film Festival in Lucca, Italy, London's Visions in the Nunnery, the STREETVIDEOART exhibition in Paris, France, Brooklyn's Ende Tymes Festival, and the Video Art and Experimental Film Festival at Tribeca Cinemas in New York City. His work has been featured in publications including Mexico City's Blancopop; Paris' Stigmart 10 – Videofocus; LandEscape Art Review and the online audio publication, Text Sound. Peterson develops and teaches courses at the School of the Art Institute of Chicago, Snow City Arts and Alphonsus Academy & Center for the Arts.

Mikey Peterson은 시카고 기반의 비디오-오디오 예술가이자 싱어송라이터이며 예술 교육자이다. 그의 작업은 시카고 현대 사진 미술관, 시카고 문화 센터, 시카고 대학의 스마트 미술관, 로마의 MAXXI 미술관, 캘리포니아 패서디나의 the Amory Center for The Arts, 시애틀의 노스웨스트 필름 포럼, 캘리포니아 로스앤젤레스에서 진행된 시그라프 콘퍼런스; 이탈리아의 루카 영화제, 런던의 Visions in the Nunnery, 파리의 STREETVIDEOART 전시, 브루클린의 Ende Tymes 페스티벌, 뉴욕 트리베카 시네마스에서 진행된 VAEFF 영상 예술 & 실험 영화제에 전시되었다. 그의 작품은 멕시코 시티의 Blancopop, 파리의 Stigmart 10- Videofocus, LandEscape Art Review와 온라인 오디오 출판사인 Text Sound에 소개되었다. 피터슨은 School of the Art Institute of Chicago와 Snow City Arts, Alphonsus Academy & Center for the Arts에서 수업을 개발하고 가르친다.

PAT REYNOLDS

Thoughts on Post-Photographic Simulation, originally written to accompany the real-fake.org.2.0 at BronxArtSpace, November 2016

By Pat Reynolds

The subjects of "photography" and what is referred to within the context of the real-fake.org.2.0 as "post-photographic simulation" (artworks created, at least in part, through the use of various specialized 3D rendering and animation softwares, but presented as still images, and often made physical through the same printing technologies and techniques used in "traditional" contemporary photographic works) have seen little crossover regarding their institutional and critical reception and presentation within the art world. Artist, author, and Rhizome founder Mark Tribe applies the term "new media art" to "projects that make use of emerging media technologies and are concerned with the cultural, political, and aesthetic possibilities of these tools," which he further defines as work operating within the intersection of "Art and Technology and Media art."1 It is potentially this self-reflexive preoccupation with the virtual that is embedded within much simulated photography that has lead to its continued categorization among new media works, rather than it being primarily defined as a tangential or sub-categorical photographic form.

The art-historical photographic narrative seems to insist that Photography, in the purest sense of the word, must involve the transmission of "real," physical light - whether through a lens, or an aperture, or a direct surface-to-surface transfer, or a gridded series or sensors programmed to translate varying intensities of electromagnetic radiation into numerical digital information — into some sort of image or transformed surface. This attachment to the physical is reflected on an institutional level not only within the basic curricula of photography programs at colleges and universities internationally, but also among contemporary art museums and galleries seeking to both define and legitimize cutting-edge and post-photographic practices. MoMA Chief Curator of Photography Quentin Bajac describes the museum's ongoing New Photography series of exhibitions as encompassing "framed prints, images on screens, commercial books, self-published books, zines, posters, photo-based installations and videos, and site-specific works," further noting that the series of exhibitions "will continue to present all the different forms that the photographic image can take."2 Still, as of the exhibition's 2015 edition, New Photography has yet to feature any work that overtly utilizes 3D simulation. Similar approaches to identifying the next wave of photographic presentation and production can be seen within the International Center of Photography's 2014 What Is a Photograph? Exhibition, the artists in which, according to its press release, "have … confronted an unexpected revolution in the medium with the rise of digital technology, which has resulted in imaginative reexaminations of the art of analog photography, the new world of digital images, and the hybrid creations of both systems as they come together."3 In this case as well, the exhibition, which aimed to trace the evolution of contemporary photography from the 1970s to the present, stopped just short of observable digital simulation in its curated works.

It is tempting to preserve the presence of the

physical in defining "true" forms of photographic practice as an ongoing recognition of photography's purely analog origins. However, the movement toward a fully simulated working environment and suite of tools could also be argued as simply the next in a historically established (and ongoing) series of steps marking photography's technological evolution. For nearly as long as photography has existed past the point of trial-and-error experimentation, a definitive constant that has persisted alongside the presence of physical light has been the photographic apparatus, which also serves as the model for the foundational set of digital tools and parameters embedded within much professional 3D simulation software. Because these pieces of software have been developed over time for advertising, filmmaking, and commercial imaging industries, the user interfaces employed within each program often employ a vocabulary that borrows from the workflows of these sorts of productions. Users, in many cases, must choose a camera with a lens of a defined focal length, and they must place it within the same three-dimensional space as their eventual photographic subject, which must also be lit using a variety of controllable light sources. They define whether or not they want to shoot an uncompressed or compressed image, and after creating an exposure, they can reframe their shot or relight their subject. With the exception of the presence of physical subjects and physical light, this process contains no more artifice than that of the contemporary studio photography shoot, which similarly consists of a defined composition of a chosen model in a customizable space lit by artificial and controllable sources and output as a generic digital file. Even simulated photographic work that eschews the laborious lighting and rendering processes of programs like Maya and Blender, such as Tribe's own Rare Earth series of landscapes from war video games or Clement Valla's Postcards From Google Earth, often exists as the product of one of a number of creative motivations typically attributed to photographers — archival impulses, seeking a so-called "decisive moment", recording a time and place in history, et cetera.

The degree to which post-photographic simulation should be considered a form of photography or a distinct new media practice, like many other nontraditional and technologically informed approaches to the medium, will undoubtedly change over time, especially as the interfaces through which artists engage with the technology continue to evolve. The representation of the typical camera system as a means of organizing the 3D workflow is currently a defining element of software like Maya, but it is also tied to present-day computer technologies and the interfaces through which we engage with them. As augmented reality and other new forms of hardware emerge in accessible consumer technologies, the approaches that artists take in the creation and presentation of 3D works will likely shift as well, presumably in a way that will lead to similar discussions of the delineation between traditional and new 3D modes of production.

Pat Reynolds, *Reflecting Pool 3* (2017)

Pat Reynolds, *Circulation* (2014), still image from digital video

포스트-포토그래피적 시뮬레이션에 대한 고찰:
2016년 11월 BronxArtSpace의 real-fake.org.2.0. 전시를 위해 작성됨

Pat Reynolds

'사진'이라는 주제와 real-fake.org.2.0.의 맥락에서 "포스트-사진 시뮬레이션"(적어도 부분적으로는 다양한 특별 3D 렌더링과 애니메이션 소프트웨어의 사용을 통해 제작되었지만 여전히 이미지로 보여지는, 그리고 종종 "전통적인" 동시대 포토그래피 작업에 사용되는 똑같은 프린팅 기술과 기법을 통해 물질적으로 만들어지는 미술 작품을 뜻한다)이 의미하는 것은 미술계 안에서 그것들이 보여지는 방식에 있어서나, 그것들의 평판을 고려했을 때 겹치는 부분이 아주 적다. 작가이자 저자, 그리고 리좀의 창시자인 마크 트라이브(Mark Tribe)는 '뉴 미디어 아트'라는 용어를 "새로운 미디어 기술을 활용하고 이러한 도구의 문화적, 정치적, 미적 가능성과 관련 있는 프로젝트"에 적용한다. 더 나아가, 그는 이 프로젝트를 "예술과 기술과 미디어 아트의 교차점에서 작동하는 작품"으로 정의한다. 이것은 잠재적으로, 뉴미디어 작품들 가운데에 지속된 범주화를 이끄는 모조된 포토그래피 안에 박힌, 가상이 있는 자기반영적인 집착이다. 우선적으로 별로 관계가 없거나 하위 범주에 있는 포토그래피 형식으로 정의되기보다 말이다.

미술사적인 사진의 내러티브는 사진이, 가장 순수한 단어의 의미에서, 어떤 종류의 이미지나 변형된 표면에 "실제" 물리적 빛이 전달되는 것과 관련 있어야 한다고 강조하는 듯 보인다 – 렌즈나 구멍, 표면간 직접 전송, 전자기 방사선의 다양한 강도를 디지털 정보 수치로 변환하도록 프로그래밍 된 그리드의 연속 또는 센서를 통해서 말이다. 이런 물리적인 것에 대한 애착은 국제적으로 대학에서 진행하는 사진 프로그램의 기본 커리큘럼 안에서뿐만 아니라 최첨단 및 포스트-포토그래피 실습을 정의하고 합법화하려는 현대미술관 및 갤러리에 걸쳐 제도적 단계에서 반영된다. 뉴욕 현대미술관 (MoMA)에서 포토그래피 분야 수석 큐레이터인 Quentin Bajac은 미술관에서 진행 중인 "뉴 포토그래피" 시리즈 전시를 "액자 인쇄물, 화면에 나오는 이미지, 상업용 서적, 자체 출판서적, 잡지, 포스터, 사진기반 설치 및 비디오 및 특정 사이트 작품"을 아우른다고 설명했으며, 일련의 전시회가 "사진 이미지가 취할 수 있는 다른 모든 형태를 계속 선보일 것이다"라고 언급했다. 그러나 뉴 포토그래피 시리즈는 2015년 판 전시회까지 3D 시뮬레이션을 과하게 사용한 어떤 작업도 선보인 적이 없다. 포토그래피적 제시와 제작의 다음 유형을 알아보려는 비슷한 접근은 국제 사진센터 (International Center of Photography)의 2014년 *사진이란 무엇인가?* 전시회에서 찾아볼 수 있다. 보도 기사에 따르면 이 전시의 작가들은 디지털 기술의 등장으로 예상치 못한 혁명에 직면했으며, 이것은 아날로그 포토그래피 예술의 창의적인 재검토와 디지털 이미지의 새로운 세상, 그리고 그것들이 함께 나타나면서 등장한 두 시스템의 혼합적인 창조로 나타났다. 1970년대부터 현재에 이르기까지 현대 사진의 진화를 추적하고자 하는 이 전시회의 경우에도 큐레이팅 된 작품에서 관측 가능한 디지털 시뮬레이션에 불과했다.

"진실된" 형태의 포토그래피적 행위를 포토그래피의 순수한 아날로그적 기원으로 정의함에 있어서 물리적인 것의 존재함을 유지하는 것은 솔깃해 보인다. 그러나, 완전히 시뮬레이션된 작업 환경과 도구로 향한 이동은 역사적으로 확립된 (그리고 확립 중인) 일련의 사진기술의 진화 단계에서 단순히 다음의 것으로 주장될 수 있다. 포토그래피가 시행착오 적 실험의 시점을 지나 존재해온 기간만큼, 물리적인 빛의 존재와 함께 계속되는 결정적인 불변은 포토그래피적 장치이며, 이는 또한 디지털 도구의 기본적인 세트를 위한 모델과 전문적인 3D 시뮬레이션의 역할을 한다. 이 소프트웨어들이 광고, 영화제작, 상업 이미지 업계에서 시간이 지남에 따라 발전되었기 때문에 각 프로그램에 사용된 사용자 인터페이스는 종종 그러한 종류의 제작 과정에서 차용한 어휘를 사용한다. 대부분의 경우 사용자는 초점 거리가 정해진 렌즈가 장착된 카메라를 선택해야 하며 최종 촬영대상과 동일한 3차원 공간 내에 배치한다. 이 촬영대상은 다양한 제어 가능한 광원을 사용하여 밝혀야 한다. 사용자는 압축된 이미지를 촬영할지 아니면 그렇지 않은 이미지를 촬영할지 선택하고, 노출도 조절한 후, 화면을 다시 구성하거나 피사체에 조명을 비출 수 있다. 물리적인 사물과 빛의 존재는 제외하고, 이 과정은 동시대 스튜디오 포토그래피 촬영 기계 이상의 기계를 포함하지 않는다. 이는 인위적이고 제어 가능한 소스에 의해 켜지고 일반 디지털 파일로 출력되며 사용자가 정의 가능한 공간에서, 선택된 모델의 정의된 구성으로 유사하게 이루어져 있다. 마야(Maya)와 블렌더(Blender) 같은 프로그램의 번거로운 조명 및 렌더링 프로세스를 피하는 시뮬레이션 된 사진작업, 예를 들어 전쟁 비디오 게임에서 나온 트라이브의 레어 어스(Rare Earth) 풍경 시리즈나 구글 어스가 만든 클레멘트 발라(Clement Valla) 엽서와 같은 작업조차도 종종 사진작가에게 기인한 많은 창의적인 동기 중 하나의 결과물로 존재한다—소위 "결정적인 순간"을 찾고, 역사 안의 시간과 장소를 기록하는 등의 기록의 충동들 말이다.

포스트-포토그래픽 시뮬레이션이 어느 정도까지 사진의 형태로, 또는, 다른 많은 비전통적이고 기술적으로 잘 아는 매체로의 접근들과 같이, 뚜렷한 뉴미디어 행위로 간주하여야 하는지는 분명히 시간이 지나면서 바뀔 것이다. 특히 작가들이 인터페이스를 통해 기술과 관여하는 것이 계속 변화하는 것처럼 말이다. 3D 작업방식을 구성하는 수단으로서의 전형적인 카메라 시스템의 재현은 현재, 마야와 같은 소프트웨어의 정의 요소일 뿐만 아니라, 오늘날의 컴퓨터 기술과 인터페이스로 연결되어 있다. 증강현실과 다른 새로운 형태의 하드웨어가 접근 가능한 소비자 기술로 등장함에 따라, 예술가가 3D 작품을 제작하고 보여주는 접근 방식도 아마 전통적인 3D 생산 방식과 새로운 3D 생산 방식 간의 구분에 대한 유사한 논의로 이어질 것이다.

Pat Reynolds is an artist, writer, and musician whose work uses digital and photographic tools to explore themes of bodily isolation, experiential alienation, and the passage of time. He is particularly interested in how we use lens-based visual media and simulation technologies to engage with both ourselves and one another. In addition to presenting work in exhibitions internationally, Pat's recent projects have included co-curating the group exhibition the real-fake.org.2.0 alongside Claudia Hart and Rachel Clarke; co-founding Pureland, an interdisciplinary publishing imprint and digital arts space, with fellow artists Jen Choi, Hannah Coleman, and Divya Gadangi; and releasing multiple music projects, including a split cassette with the Providence-based musician Big Nice. Pat studied film production and photography as an undergraduate at Emerson College in Boston, Massachusetts, and he received his Master's degree in Visual and Critical Studies from the School of the Art Institute of Chicago. He currently lives and works in Brooklyn, New York.

Pat Reynolds는 아티스트이자 저자 및 음악가로, 신체적 고립, 경험적 소외감 및 흐르는 시간을 탐색하기 위해 디지털과 사진 도구를 사용한다. 그는 특히 렌즈 기반의 시각 매체 사용법과 시뮬레이션 기술을 사용해 자신 스스로와 타인과의 관계에 주목하는 데에 관심이 있다. 최근에는 국제 전시회에서 작품을 발표할 뿐만 아니라 Claudia Hart과 Rachel Clarke와 함께 그룹 전시회 real-fake.org.2.0를 큐레이팅했다. 또한 아티스트 Jen Choi, Hannah Coleman, Divya Gadangi와 함께 출판사이자 디지털 아트 공간인 Pureland를 설립하였다. 그리고 본인의 지역색을 녹여 작업하는 음악가 Big Nice와 함께 한 조각 카세트 등 여러 음악 프로젝트를 발표했다. Pat은 보스턴 Emerson College에서 영화 제작과 사진 촬영을 전공했고 the School of the Art Institute of Chicago에서 시각 비평학 석사 학위를 이수했다. 현재 뉴욕 브루클린에서 거주하며 작품 활동을 하고 있다.

MIKE RICHISON

Video VotoMatic combines a drum sequencer and a vintage voting machine. The interface samples footage from the current presidential race and allows a user to sequence several individual video tracks on a sixteen-beat loop. The software was patterned after the legendary Roland TR 808 drum machine. Users punch their rhythm into a "voting booklet" that mimics the infamous punch card-style Votomatic voting machines used during the 2000 Florida election debacle. Instead of a providing the names of candidates, the booklet is filled with sample drum patterns.

Users can follow the patterns suggested by the booklet or they can punch in their own. The piece samples words, phrases, breaths, pauses, and other sounds and silences in order to build percussion tracks, melodies, and solos, creating a breakdown of language. Several stations exist, and an installation would closely resemble a real-life polling station, resulting in an uncanny experience for the participant.

In addition to being a commentary on the contemporary politics and news coverage thereof, this installation is a study of information design. *Video VotoMatic* attempts to collect the raw material of news footage and give the user a visual means of breaking down the material. Both the booklet (with its tablature of rhythmic patterns) – and the screen's user interface (displaying a 16 or 32 beat loop) allow for a new interpretation, or metamorphosis of the video and speech of the candidates. The stump speeches and canned deliveries become broken down into rhythms, beats and loops.

*Video VotoMatic*은 드럼 시퀀서와 빈티지 투표 기계를 결합해 만든 것이다. 인터페이스는 대선 장면을 샘플링하고 사용자가 16 비트 루프에서 여러 개별 비디오 트랙을 편집할 수 있게 해준다. 이 소프트웨어는 전설적인 Roland TR 808 드럼 머신을 따라 제작됐다. 사용자는 소책자에 리듬을 펀치로 뚫어 새긴다. 이는 악명높은 2000년 미국 대선 중 플로리다 선거전 당시의 악명 높은 Votomatic 투표 기계를 모방한 것이다. 후보자의 이름 대신 소책자는 드럼 패턴으로 채워진다.

사용자는 소책자에 나와 있는 패턴을 따르거나 자신만의 패턴을 펀치로 뚫어 만들 수 있다. 이 곡은 언어를 분해하며 타악기 트랙, 멜로디, 솔로를 만들기 위해 단어, 구문, 숨소리, 일시 중지 및 기타 소리와 정적을 샘플링한다. 여러 개의 기계가 실제 투표소와 매우 유사하게 배치되어 있어 참여자에게 이상한 경험을 하게 한다.

본 작품은 현대 정치와 뉴스 보도에 대한 비판과 동시에 정보 디자인 대한 연구이다. *Video VotoMatic*은 원 보도 자료를 수집하며 사용자에게 자료를 분해할 수 있는 시각적 수단을 제공한다. 소책자 (리디미컬한 패턴의 악보)와 화면으로 보는 사용자 인터페이스 (16 혹은 32비트 루프를 보여줌)은 후보자의 영상과 음성의 새로운 해석 또는 변형을 유도한다. 정치 연설과 이의 녹음본은 리듬, 비트, 루프로 쪼개진다.

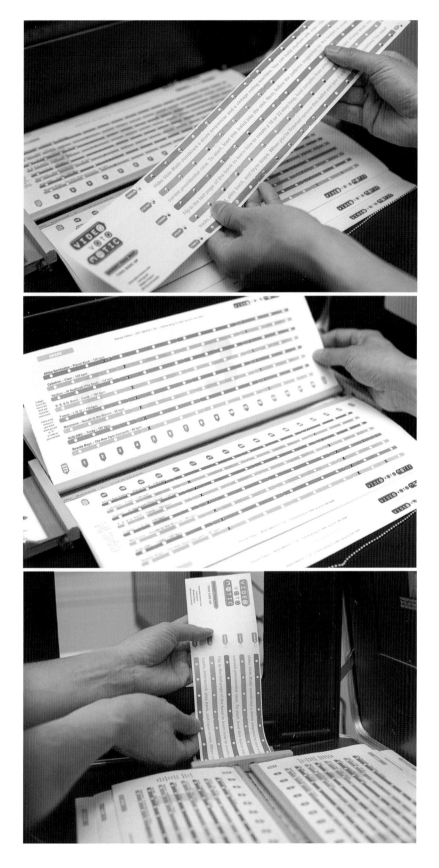

Mike Richison, *Video Voto Matic* (2016)

After calling the Detroit, Michigan area home for a number of years, Mike Richison relocated to New Jersey in 2007. He is currently a professor at Monmouth University where he teaches motion graphics and graphic design. He is a multimedia artist who has exhibited and performed at venues and galleries within the US and internationally.

Mike Richison은 수년간 미시간주에 살다 디트로이트에 취직 후, 2007년 뉴저지로 이전했다. 현재 그는 Monmouth University에서 모션 그래픽과 그래픽 디자인과 교수이다. 그는 멀티미디어 아티스트이며 미국과 해외에서 공연 및 전시를 해왔다.

Mike Richison, *Video Voto Matic* (2016)

ELISSAVET SFYRI

Practicing

A live sculpture installation and performance which consists of a moving platform that produces sounds according to the rhythmic movement of the bodies standing on it. Contact microphones are attached to the moving platform and onto the body, capturing even the slightest sound, in order to create a loud sound collage within the exhibition space, using both the body and the platform as instruments.

The concept is the "deconstruction" of the human body, and its transformation into a space of experiences with emphasis on an unconventional use of sound. This separates and at the same time brings back together time and space into one dimension.

This piece explores how our ideas and thoughts exist way before our bodies come to life, through past generations. The body is screaming to escape its own self and society, while at the same time it is living and dying for previous and next generations.

"The scream is not yours. It is not you who speaks; it is your countless ancestors. It is not you who craves; countless generations of ancestors crave through your own heart.

Your dead are not lying in the ground. They have turned into birds, and trees, and wind. You sit in their shade, eat their flesh, and breathe their breath. They have become ideas and passions and master your will and actions.

Future generations do not move in uncertainty far from you. They live, act and desire in your lungs and heart."

훈련

리드미컬한 몸동작에 따라 사운드를 만들어내는 움직이는 플랫폼으로 구성된 조각 설치 미술과 공연. 움직이는 플랫폼과 몸에 부착된 콘택트 마이크는 사소한 소리까지 잡아내고, 몸과 플랫폼을 악기로 사용해 전시 공간 안의 큰 사운드 콜라주를 만들어낸다.

이 작업의 개념은 몸의 "해체"와 사운드의 비관습적 활용에 역점을 둔 경험 공간으로의 변형이다. 이는 시간과 공간을 분리하고 동시에 다시 한 차원으로 융합시킨다.

이 작품은 우리의 몸이 생기기 전 우리의 생각들이 과거 세대를 통해 어떻게 존재하는지를 탐구한다. 신체는 자신과 사회를 벗어나기 위해 비명을 지르고 있는 동시에 이전과 이후 세대를 위해 죽음과 삶을 반복한다.

"비명은 네 것이 아니다. 말하는 것은 네가 아니다. 네 수많은 조상이다. 네가 갈망하는 것이 아니다. 셀 수 없이 많은 세대의 조상이 네 마음을 통해 갈망한 것이라.

너의 죽은 사람들은 땅에 눕지 않는다. 그들은 새와 나무, 바람으로 변해왔다. 너는 그들의 그늘에 앉고, 그들의 살을 먹고, 그들의 숨을 쉰다. 그들은 지혜와 열정이 되어 너의 의지와 행동을 관철한다.

자손들은 너에게서 먼 불확실한 곳으로 가지 않을 것이다. 그들은 네 폐와 심장 속에 살며 행동하고 열망할 것이다."

Elissavet Sfyri, *Practicing* (2016), stills from video documentation of live sculpture performance

Elissavet Sfyri, *Practicing* (2016), still from video documentation of live sculpture performance

Elissavet Sfyri는 런던에 기반을 둔 그리스 예술가이다. 그녀는 2016년 6월에 Gold-smiths University of London에서 순수 예술 학사 수료했고, 2017년 9월 Royal College of Arts에서 조소 석사 과정을 시작했다.

"훈련을 통해 여러 무대를 거치며, 장르를 넘나드는 것을 좋아한다. 내가 어떠한 장르에 속하는지 정확히 알 수는 없지만 내 작업을 관철하는 주제들이 있다. 나는 관객들의 '인간의 여러 겹의 다양한 면'을 '벗기고,' 나약함과 권위 게임을 청중들과 한계를 시험하는 것을 좋아한다. 나는 인체를 매체이자 주제로 다루며, 소리를 통해 시간과 공간을 '유린'한다.

나는 살아 움직이는 몸과 움직이지 않는 물체들의 상호 작용을 담은 내 작품을 살아있는 조각이라고 생각한다. 인체는 끊임없이 수백만의 소리를 만들고 외부로 발산하는 살아있는 조각이라고 생각한다."

Elissavet Sfyri is a Greek artist based in London. She graduated from Goldsmiths University of London BA Fine Art in June 2016. In September 2017 she will be starting her MA course in Sculpture at the Royal College of Arts.

"Having gone through multiple stages in my practice, I like to work across (clashing) genres and although one cannot pinpoint where my practice lies, there are themes that distinguish it. I like to 'denude' my audience of their various 'human layers,' and push their limits and my own, through vulnerability and games of authority; I use the human body both as medium and subject; I often 'ravage' time and space through sound.

I think of many of my artworks as live sculptures, because of the interactions of living bodies with inanimate objects. I consider the human body to be a live sculpture, constantly producing millions of sounds and externalizing them."

MATT SHERIDAN

INTERVIEW: Matt Sheridan speaking with Willoughby Rockwell

about Matsudo: Ebb+Flow, 2015

You call your video animations "paintings-in-motion." Why use abstract painting as a basis for video production?

Animation is a cinematic medium defined by narrative depictions giving an illusion of life. My work does not present an illusion of life. Rather, it expands perceptions of movement in painted, non-narrative images actualizing those perceived movements into real-time actions which may be mechanically, organically and/or materially-driven. "Painting-in-motion" refers to the movement of my hand-painted marks, technological delivery systems and performative aspects of my work, which is essentially action painting sequentialized into the expanded field of video. I've always viewed abstract painting as an entry point into imaginary space. Video physicalizes that imaginary space via projections, so now anyone can step into an immersive space of painting. Abstract action painting is my particular point of departure, so the idea is to extend bodily instinct from objects of painting – where the body is in control – into experiences of painting, where the painting-in-motion is in control. Perceptions of actions in spaces of abstract painting generally begin as questions regarding surfaces and supports, where photographic perceptions realistically depict the world according to recorded, recognizable images. My work allows viewers to flip the script in both circumstances to create a third way to experience the work as art.

Tell me the origin of Matsudo: Ebb+Flow (2015)?

Previously I made a work called *Chasing Tail* (2011) which I projected exclusively on architectural supports – facades and interiors – on five continents. *Chasing Tail* was the prototype for *Matsudo: Ebb+Flow* because its locations prompted the following questions: What if painting-in-motion projection is limited only to interior spaces? How might I integrate my work into domestic life without the weight of public spectacle? How might people respond to it? If limited to interior domestic spaces in one specific region, how might projection both carry and relate characteristics of many faces in that particular place? Finally, how could I edit a videographic documentation of the work to function as a cinematic portrait, as a work-in-itself? So I wanted this work to spotlight comparisons and contrasts in all the interiors it was projected.

Why Japan?

My very limited, Americanized experience of Japanese culture is an observation of rich inner lives obscured by facades and expectations of propriety, formality, respect and elegance. Another observation - having lived in Singapore for a year-and-a-half - was that the Japanese have, in comparison, a more intuitively inventive sense of personal style and fashion than other places I've traveled such as China and Singapore, where there exists a more "off-the-rack" "designer-name" mentality minus mixing and matching to sit one's own taste and aesthetic. I wanted to test that observation by assimilating my work into everyday Japanese life to see how both might change. That was my pitch to the Paradise AIR curators and town council, who were open to the idea.

That sounds like a dangerous dance with colonialism?!

Projecting a "white American attitude" into foreign locations is always the pitfall I aim to avoid. If I am a guest in other countries and while I'm there, the one who gets colonized is me! My goal is always to assimilate culture into my work – and vice versa -- to continue, extend or differently illuminate conversations already happening in other nations as apolitically as possible by using abstraction to explore ideas present in those countries. In Matsudo, a starting point for conversation was the town's history as a meeting point for travelers en route to Tokyo. I applied for Paradise AIR specifically because of their theme for the residency – HERE. As advertised, The idea was for artists to make work in a former love hotel in a town where the townspeople wanted to learn more about, better understand and appreciate contemporary art, recognizing an opportunity to see the world differently after the 2011 tsunami. A kind of transactional blankness was put into effect. Since I knew little about the town, who presented themselves to me as a "blank canvas" for my work, I had to learn about them quickly over the limited period of the residency, 10 weeks.

What DID you learn while making this work?

I learned a great deal in Matsudo which I apply to my work even now. A number of translated conversations with Matsudo's people enlightened me very early on in my residency. One person asked me if I would make an animated shape for Matsudo, to which I said yes. He responded "Then it's gonna SUCK!" before draining his beer. I took that as a personal challenge while recognizing the population's common anxiety regarding their relationship to contemporary art. I later found a serenity in the townspeople that I abstracted into a second shape in Matsudo: Ebb+Flow. Both abstractions underline these interwoven tendencies in Matsudo's residents, hence the work's title. It's my hope that Matsudo: Ebb+Flow celebrates and universalizes shared characteristics between Matsudo's townspeople and viewers of all nationalities.

When not hang gliding off the peaks of Rio de Janeiro, motorcycling through South India or draining dirty vodka martinis like they were iced tea in Helsinki, Willoughby Rockwell occupies his idle time perusing the art world as if it were a location worth visiting. From this vantage point Rockwell works with various international artists and publications in the guise of critic, writer, provocateur and inspirational party animal. Among his eclectic projects are: an ongoing series of antagonistic letters, a short film script for a collaborative exhibition at Paris' Jeu de Paume in 2011, an artist profile written in 2012 for New Delhi's Take On Art magazine and a 2014 festival projection near his beach shack in Malibu, California.

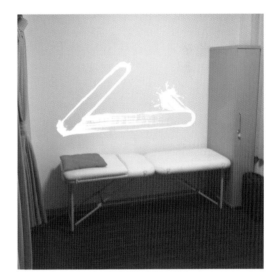

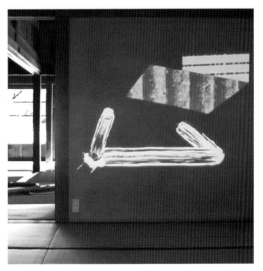

Matt Sheridan, *Matsudo Ebb + Flow at Daiei Mall* (2015) (top),
Matsudo Ebb + Flow at Radio Poireau (2015) (middle),
Matsudo Ebb + Flow at Tojo Tei (2015) (bottom)

인터뷰: Matsudo: Ebb+Flow (2015) 작품

Willoughby Rockwell 진행

본인이 작업한 비디오 애니메이션을 "움직이는 그림"이라고 했는데, 추상화를 영상 제작의 기반으로 사용한 이유가 무엇인가?

애니메이션은 영화적 매체로, 서사적인 묘사로 삶의 환영을 보여준다. 내 작품은 삶의 환영을 보여주지는 않는다. 대신 기계적, 자연적, 또는 물질적으로 발생하는 실시간의 움직임을 채색된 비서사적인 이미지에 적용해 이를 동적 영역으로 확장한다. "움직이는 그림"은 내가 직접 그린 흔적의 움직임과 영상의 영역으로 확장된 액션 페인팅인 내 작업의 기술적 전달 및 구현 방식에 관해 다룬다. 나는 언제나 추상화를 상상의 공간으로 들어가는 입구로 보았다. 영상은 프로젝터 투사를 통해 가상 공간을 실제화함으로 이제는 누구나 몰입형 가상 공간 회화를 시도할 수 있다. 추상 액션 페인팅은 나의 출발점이고, 몸을 제어하는 것으로 부터 움직이는 회화를 제어하는 경험으로 확장된다. 보통 사진학적 지각이 현실적으로 세계를 기록하고 인지할 수 있는 이미지로 묘사되는 반면, 추상화 공간 속에서 동작에 대한 인식은 표면과 지지대에 대한 질문으로 시작한다. 여기서. 내는 관객들이 기존의 방법보다는 새로운 방식으로 예술 작품을 경험할 수 있게 유도한다.

마츠도: Ebb+Flow (2015)는 어떻게 시작하게 되었나?

이전에 Chasing Tail (2011)이라는 작품에서 5대륙 모습을 건축적 구조물에 투사했었다. Chasing Tail은 Matsudo: Ebb+Flow의 시범작으로 다음 질문들을 던지게 했다. 영상을 실내 공간에만 투사하면 어떨까? 어떻게 내 작업을 공공 공간이 아닌 내 개인적 삶의 영역과 통합시킬까? 관객들이 어떻게 반응할까? 투사를 특정 지역의 실내 공간으로 국한할 경우, 어떻게 그 장소의 많은 면의 특성을 반영할 수 있을까? 마지막으로, 작품을 비디오 다큐멘터리로 찍어서 그 자체로 영상 초상화와 같은 작품을 만들면 어떨까? 이런 이유로 집 안의 모든 곳에 영상을 투사해 비교해보며 작품을 발전시켰다.

왜 일본인가?

미국인으로서의 일본 문화의 경험은 물론 제한적이었지만 정당성과 형식, 존중과 우아함에 대해 기대감으로 감춰진 풍부한 영적 생활에 대해 관찰했다. 싱가포르에서 1년 반 동안 살면서 일본인이 중국이나 싱가포르 같은 곳보다 더 직관적이고 독창적인 스타일과 패션 감각을 가졌다는 생각이 들었다. 중국이나 싱가포르 사람들은 자신의 취향과 미적 감각에 맞추기 위해 믹싱과 매칭하기 보다는 "기성품"이나 "디자이너 이름"을 선호하는 듯했다. 이런 일본인의 일상생활에 내 작업을 동화시키면서 두 가지가 어떻게 변하는지 시험하고 싶었다. 이 아이디어을 Paradise Air 큐레이터와 시 의회에 이 아이디어를 제안했었고 긍정적 반응을 얻었다.

식민주의와 위험한 줄타기를 하는 것 같이 들린다만?!

"백인 미국인의 태도"를 외국에 투사하려는 것은 내가 항상 피하려고 하는 부분이다. 만일 내가 다른 나라의 손님이고 그곳에 있다면, 식민지배 당하는 사람은 나이다! 나는 문화를 내 작업에 반영하고 내 작업 또한 문화에 반영하고자 한다. 더 나아가 다른 국가에서도 이를 진행하며 추상화 작업을 거쳐 최대한 정치적이지 않으려고 노력한다. 마츠도에서는, 도쿄로 가는 여행자들이 만나는 지점인 마을의 역사에서 대화가 시작되었다. Paradise AIR에서 "HERE" 라는 주제의 레지던스 공모를 보고 주제가 마음에 들어 신청하게 되었다. 지역주민에게 현대미술을 이해하고 감상할 기회를 주고 2011년 쓰나미 이후 세상을 다르게 볼 수있는 기회를 주기위해 러브 호텔을 개조하여 아티스트 레지던스 프로그램을 개발한 것이다. 이를 통해 일종의 공백을 제공한 셈이다. 그들은 나의 작업의 "빈 캔버스"가 되고자 했고 나는 10주에 거쳐 빠르게 마을에 관해 배워야 했다.

이 작업을 하며 무엇을 배웠나

마츠도에서 많은 것을 배웠고, 이는 현재 내 작업에 반영되고 있다. 레지던스 초기 마츠도 사람들과 나눴던 대화들은 매우 감명 깊었다. 한 분이 마츠도를 위한 형태 애니메이션을 만들 수 있는지 물었고, 나는 그렇다고 말했다. 그는 맥주를 벌컥벌컥 마시며 전 "그렇담 형편없겠네!"라고 답했다. 난 그 말을 개인적인 도전으로 받아들였고, 주민들이 현대미술을 갑자기 마주하며 느끼는 공통적인 불안에 대해서도 인지했다. 시간 지나 마츠도 주민들에게 "Matsudo: Ebb+Flow"의 두번째 추상화된 형태를 보여주었을 때 그들이 부쩍 현대 작품에 익숙해지고 편안해졌음을 느꼈다. 두 추상화는 마츠도 주민들의 이러한 경향들을 반영하고, 작품의 제목도 이를 바탕으로

지었다. Matsudo: Ebb+Flow를 통해 마을 사람들과 국제 관객들 모두 공통된 특징을 향유하고 축하하는 장이 되었으면 한다.

리오 데 자네이루의 봉우리에서 글라이딩 할 때, 남부 인도를 가로지르며 모터 사이클을 탈 때, 헬싱키에서 보드카 마티니를 아이스티처럼 들이킬 때, 이런 시간 외에 한가할 때 Willoughby Rockwell은 가치 있는 곳을 여행하듯이 예술 세계에 심취한다. Rockwell은 비평가, 작가, 선동가, 또한 영감을 주는 파티 중독자로서 수많은 국제 작가 및 출판 작업에 동참했다. 그의 다양한 프로젝트는 현재 진행 중인 적대적 편지 시리즈, 2011년 파리 Jeu de Paume 협업 전시를 위한 단편 영화 대본, 뉴 델리 Take On Art 잡지를 위해 2012년에 쓰인 작가 프로필 및 2014년 캘리포니아 말리부 그의 해변 오두막집 근처에서 열린 프로젝션 축제가 있다.

Matt Sheridan은 로스앤젤레스 기반의 예술가로 추상 비디오와 페인트 작업을 한다. 뉴욕 대학교 티시 예술대학부에서 미술학사 학위를 얻었고 캘리포니아에 위치한 패서디나 아트 센터 디자인 대학교에서 석사를 이수했다. 수많은 수상 경력과 장학금, 아티스트 레지던시 수령자로 Sheridan은 5개 대륙을 넘어 세계적으로 전시한다. 2016년에 그는 뉴욕과 브리즈번 호주에서 개인전을 선보였고 그의 작품을 개인 소장하고 있는 로스앤젤레스 도시 곳곳의 단체전에 참여했다. 또한, 그는 LA에 기반을 둔 힙합 댄스 회사인 Antics Performance를 위해 페인팅-인-모션 비디오 배경을 기획했는데, 이는 Sneaker Suites라는 이름의 미국 투어에서 사용되었다. 2017년 Sheridan은 마이애미에서 단체전 및 비디오 퍼포먼스와 로스앤랜젤레스에서 몇 개의 단체전 및 아티스트 레지던시에 참여했다. 또한, TW Fine Art in Brisbane에서 열린 개인전을 통해 회화와 영상 작품을 소개했다.

Matt Sheridan is a Los Angeles-based artist who makes abstract videos and paintings. He earned his BFA from NYU/Tisch School of the Arts and his MFA from Art Center College of Design in Pasadena, California. A recipient of numerous awards, grants, fellowships and artist residencies, Sheridan exhibits globally across five continents. In 2016 he exhibited in solo shows in New York and Brisbane Australia and also contributed to group shows in Los Angeles, all cities in which Sheridan's works are in private collections. In addition, he projected a painting-in-motion video backdrop for LA-based hip-hop dance company Antics Performance, whose production Sneaker Suites toured the US. In 2017 Sheridan is participating in a group show / video performance in Miami, several group exhibitions and an artist residency in Los Angeles, and another solo exhibition of paintings and video at TW Fine Art in Brisbane.

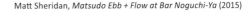

Matt Sheridan, *Matsudo Ebb + Flow at Bar Noguchi-Ya* (2015)

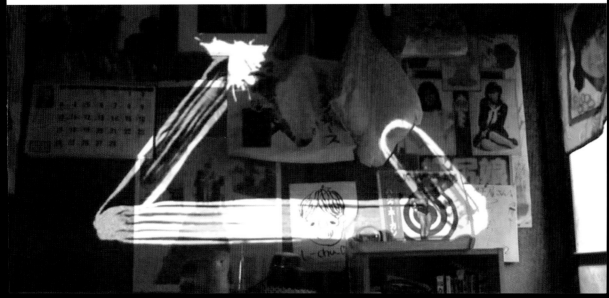

CHRISTIAN TABLAZON

Christian Tablazon, untitled diptychs from the series "Holotype" (2015–17), B/W digital photographs, dimensions variable

Christian Tablazon, untitled diptychs from the series "Holotype" (2015–17), B/W digital photographs, dimensions variable

Mostly shot using consumer-grade cameras and phased-out camera phones, "Holotype" is a series of diptychs that notate place and the human body in both the natural and fabled contexts of anthropology, natural history, geology, and architecture. These representations poised as tableau-vivant pairings aim at probing and reworking the codes and rhetoric of colonial naturalist and ethnographic discourse, offering indices to contact zones and encounters, and to the long and complex 'romance' between colonizer and indigene (and their often permeable borders) within contemporary and fictionalized images. The series seeks to explore the convolutions of representation in the name of empire and truth-making, in the blurred lines between art, science, and superstition, the relationship between epistemology and colonization, and the intimate link between fascination and violence.

"Holotype" 시리즈는 대부분 아마추어 용 카메라와 낡은 핸드폰 카메라를 사용해서 촬영했다. "Holotype" 는 인류학과 자연사, 지질학, 그리고 건축의 자연적이고 우화적인 맥락에서 장소와 인체를 기록한 두 폭 사진 시리즈이다. 이는 식민지적 박물학자와 민족 지학적 담론의 코드와 수사법들을 탐구하고 재구축하기 위한 활인화로써 묘사되었다. 이를 통해 접촉면과 조우의 지표들을 제공하고, 현대적이고 허구적인 이미지들 안에 식민 지배자와 원주민 사이의 (그리고 그들의 빈번한 투과적 경계들) 길고 복잡한 '로맨스'를 만든다. "Holotype" 시리즈는 예술과 과학, 미신의 흐릿한 경계들, 인식론과 식민지화 사이의 관계, 그리고 매혹과 폭력 사이의 친숙한 관련성 사이에서 제국의 이름과 진리의 구축이라는 이름의 재현의 난해함을 탐구한다.

Christian Tablazon (b. Manila) works mainly with mixed media, photography, and video. Together with young writers and artists in 2012, he founded The Cabinet, an artist collective and small independent press. He is a recipient of several national fellowships in creative writing and cultural criticism, and an international fellowship in transdisciplinary arts with the I-Node–Planetary Collegium of Plymouth University. He has been published and exhibited in 13 countries, and his videos were also screened as part of the second edition of The Wrong–New Digital Art Biennale. He is one of the artists selected to participate in Treviso at the fourth B#Side War Project (2018–19), an international art festival on 20th-century war legacies, and his solo exhibition comprised of video installations is also slated at the National Commission for Culture and the Arts (NCCA) Gallery in Manila late next year.

필리피니 마닐라 태생 Christian Tablazon 은 주로 텍스트, 사진 및 비디오 작업을 한다. 그는 예술, 문화 비평을 통해 여러 곳에서 국가 연구 장학금을 받았고, Plymouth University로부터 학제적 예술 분야로 국제 연구 장학금을 받았다. 그의 작품은 12개국에서 출판 및 전시되었으며, 그의 영상 작품은 The Wrong – New Digital Art Biennale에서 상영되었다.

KAMIL TATARA

Sunflowers
Repetition of the 3rd version

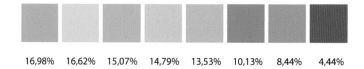

16,98%   16,62%   15,07%   14,79%   13,53%   10,13%   8,44%   4,44%

Sunflowers
4th version

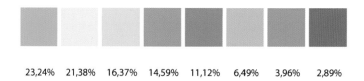

23,24%   21,38%   16,37%   14,59%   11,12%   6,49%   3,96%   2,89%

Kamil Tatara, color swatches from the series *Color Studies - Vincent* (2016)

Color Studies

Colour theories are fascinating topic for me, same as they ware for Vincent Van Gogh, back in his time. That's why I decide to start my series using his Sunflowers works, analyse them and create my own studies based on colours. It become very interesting to do such simple thing as disintegration of artwork just to see pure colour scheme and compare them to other settings made by same author, on same topic and same composition. I decide to use original Sunflowers size as in his pieces, 92x72 cm and set them together as a diptych. That way of seeing those repetition together allow us to see and compare colour compositions he have made. First thing I did was divisioning eight different major colours that are present at painting. Analyzing them using web engine colour summarizer. Next step was to convert them to NCS colour values and then use those parameters to prepare specific paint in colour laboratory. I decide to use horizontal stripes in combination as it goes from top: 2-4-6-8-7-5-3-1. Setting biggest percentage value stripe at the bottom of a painting.

Kamil Tatara, *Sunflowers Repetition of 3rd Version, Color Studies - Vincent* (2016) oil on canvas

164

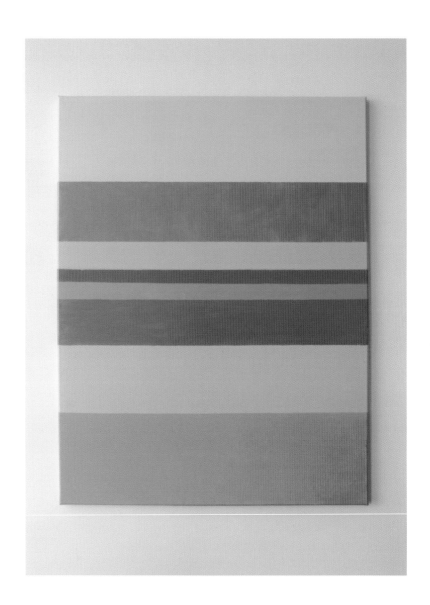

색채 연구

빈세트 반 고흐가 그랬던 것처럼 색채 이론은 매우 흥미로운 주제
이다. 이는 내가 반 고흐의 해바라기 작업을 이용하여 색채 연구
시리즈를 시작하게 된 이유이기도 하다. 이 시리즈는 반 고흐의
작품들을 분석하고, 이를 기반으로 나만의 색 연구를 만들어가
는 과정이다. 작가의 색채 조합에만 오로지 집중하며, 작가가 같
은 주제와 같은 구성으로 만들어낸 다른 색 조합들의 비교하면서
예술 작품을 분해하는 것은 단순하지만 매우 흥미로운 과정이다.
나는 반 고흐의 해바라기 원작과 같은 치수인 92x72cm 크기의
딥디크 - 둘로 접힌 한 쌍의 그림으로 이 Color Studies 시리즈를
구성하였다. 색채의 반복을 함께 보면 반 고흐가 만들어낸 색 조
합을 비교할 수 있다. 이 시리즈의 첫 단계는 반 고흐의 작품에서
우리가 볼 수 있는 8개의 서로 다른 주요 색들을 분해하는 일이
다. 색 분석은 온라인 색 요약 소프트웨어를 이용했다. 다음에는
그것들을 NCS 색상표로 변환했다. 그 후 색 연구실에 준비된 특
정한 작품들에 이 매개 변수들을 접목한다. 나는 이 색상들을 위
에서부터 실제 그림에서 각 색상이 쓰인 비율 (2-4-6-8-7-5-3-1)
로 평행선으로 병치하였다.

Kamil Tatara was born in 1981. In
2006, he recieve MFA at Universitas
Nicolai Copernici - Torun, Poland,
specializing in Drawing. Now Kamil
work and live in Poznan, Poland.
Through various media including
Paintings, Installations, and
Conceptual Art, He explores digital
aspects of human life.
www.tatarakamil.com

Kamil Tatara는 1981년에 태어났다. 폴란드
토루니의 Universitas Nicolai Copernici에
서 드로잉 전공으로 석사 학위를 받았다.
현재 폴란드 포즈나니에 거주하며 작품 활
동을 하고 있다. 그는 회화, 설치, 개념 미술
등 다양한 매체를 통해 인간 삶과 디지털의
특성을 탐구한다. www.tatarakamil.com

Kamil Tatara, *Sunflowers 4th Version, Color Studies - Vincent* (2016) oil on canvas, Profile Photo by Piotr Banaszek

JESSICA TSANG

by Miguel Arrais Pacheco

Two bodies converse in intimacy. We mostly hear the words and see the images of one single person, but this body really is the product of the dialogue between the two.

The structure of the film sets in motion distinct and sometimes opposing strategies for the manifestation of these two bodies and the connections between them. The hypervisible body that constitutes the focus of the film is the reflection of the largely invisible body of the filmmaker. By attaching different cameras to her own body, Jessica Tsang emphasizes herself as a subjective and kaleidoscopic POV peering and probing another body, as well as the editing tool that directs the rhythms and movements of the images, while all the same constituting the body on display and its spoken discourse as the centre of the narrative.

The plurality created by the filmic techniques reinforces the multiplicity put forth by the main figure on the screen. Perception itself is made multiple, both in visual and cognitive terms, in the sense that the technology used to mediate the body is materially manifested in ways that match the plurality conveyed by that same filmed body. Digital media and the proliferation of images that it is commonly associated with become both the material tools and the symbols of a body that breaks or exceeds binary norms.

We are presented with a body manifested under certain codes of femininity, but performed in a manner and shown beside a discourse that complicate both gender and biological categorization. The unnamed main character of the film voices a speech that does not seem to exactly coincide with the bodily performances we see.

The display of physical attributes of the body, the clothing, the projection of the voice, the posing of the body, all point to femininity, but a type of femininity in excess of itself. The theatricality involved in the presentation of the body and the attire worn, the dramatic intonation of the voice,

the sensually saturated poses of the body actually perform the marking of femininity with an emphasis on the artificial,which seems particularly underlined by the silver mask-like make-up covering part of the face. A certain stativity of movement, combined with the notably staged character of the scenes (the body lying on a on a bed, seating in the bathroom, standing in the kitchen), seems to contribute to this sense of the artifice.

However, it becomes clear that this visible gender performance cannot be explained away by the category of drag. That clarity is introduced by the discourse being proffered, which is complex in content and delivery, but which most of all confuses and complicates notions of fluidity and rigidity of gender and the sexed body.

Perhaps most emphasized is the defence of science as a tool for knowledge and categorization of the sexed body, defining a space beyond the binary of the female and the male. The issue is widely commented upon while only once explicitly introducing the term for the non-binary category of the intersex, or the body that encompasses both female and male biological attributes. It is here that the locus of identity of the character can be projected upon, as we understand the importance that science and biology can pose in terms of the space of intelligibility created by or for certain non-normative subjects.

But also perhaps most evident is the way in which the defence of scientific notions of the body are paired with a deconstruction of the opposition between the natural and the artificial. If the 'natural', 'scientific' body of the intersex can be said to find support in the notion of an essentialism of the non-binary sexed body, it is nonetheless manifested by a body in performance and a body that embraces and manifests artifice in the way that it conveys its gendering. The intersex body is then hinted at as a biological category that not only sits outside the female-male

binary, but more directly points to the opening of a space of gendering that is not strictly determinable in anticipation and that might result in the production of new genders.

If this space sits in the intersection of biology and gender formation, then it reflects an intersectionality that confronts and soothes possible conflicts between notions of (trans) gender supported by the queering of normative categories on one hand, and of the figuration of transsexuality as crossing strictly opposite sexed poles. In other words, the intersex body, as presented and defended in the film, creates a multiple space where the positive use of (non-binary) biological categories works in conjunction with the possibility of appropriation, resignification and new production of gendering. This conjunction is actively performed in the difference between the defence of scientific methods and categorizations in relation to the body, and the presentation of gender as beyond the natural.

We can look at the title of the film for a clue to this space that might be occupied by the body on the screen. If we take 'yes' and 'no' as polar opposites of a binary system, 'maybe' does more than define a space in between, and introduces the possibility of alternative spaces created in indeterminacy. In the film we never actually hear about the biological features of the body that we see, and there is no resolution to the issue of the 'nature' of the presentation of femininity of the character. 'Maybe' is perhaps the best category to relativize the focus on the coincidence of bodily and gendered manifestations, at the same time as it creates new meanings of the body and identity that do not conform to binary normativity.

Jessica Tsang, *Yes, No, Maybe* (2014), Installation View (top), still from digital video (bottom)

Miguel Arrais Pacheco 저

두 인물이 친밀한 대화를 나눈다. 우리는 영상을 통해 주인공의 이야기를 듣거나 그 사람의 모습을 본다. 그러나 이 영상은 실제 둘이 나누는 대화의 결과물이다.

영화 구성의 움직임은 명확히 구별되면서도 어떨 땐 두 인물의 표현이라던가 둘의 관계에 대한 전략을 틀어버리기도 한다. 영상의 중심이 되는 선명하게 묘사되는 인물은 감독의 보이지 않는 몸에 대한 반영물이다. Jessica Tsang은 여러 종류의 카메라를 자신의 몸에 부착함으로써 신체를 통해 촬영되는 관점을 강조하며 변화무쌍한 장면을 병치시키는 동시에 다른 인물을 살피고 있다. 영상이 펼쳐지며 인물이 중심 이야기를 만들어내는 동안 편집된 도구들은 이미지의 움직임과 리듬을 표현한다.

영상 기술로 만들어진 다중이미지는 중심인물을 스크린 위에 내비치면서 다양성을 강조한다.

우리의 관점은 시각적 그리고 인지적 다양성에 의해 만들어진다. 기술 발전이 몸의 사용에 영향을 미치듯 화면을 통해 보이는 몸은 다중성과 매치되며 신체는 물질적으로 표현된다. 디지털 미디어와 이미지들의 확산은 물질적 도구와 상징으로서의 몸이라는 양분된 개념을 부수거나 초월하는 방식과 관련을 맺고 있다.

특정 여성성의 코드를 통해 우리의 몸은 표현되나 행동을 하거나 보이는 몸은 복잡하게도 성적이거나 생물 학적의 범위를 넘어서 있다. 화면상의 이름 없는 주인공의 목소리는 우리가 보는 신체의 행위와는 완벽하게 조화를 이루지 않는다.

영상에 비치는 인물의 신체적 특성, 옷, 목소리, 자세 등은 여성성을 강조하나 한편으로는 여성성을 초월하는 듯도 하다. 신체의 표현, 주인공이 입고 있는 옷, 인상적인 목소리, 억양, 관능적인 포즈를 통한 연극적 행위는 여성성을 강조하는 행동으로 보이나 은색 가면을 쓴 듯한 메이크업이 온 얼굴을 뒤덮고 있는 주인공을 통해 인위적 여성성 또한 강조된다. 연극적으로 꾸며진 특정 상태의 움직임들 (예를 들어 침대에 누워있거나 화장실에 앉아있거나 주방에 서 있는 등의)은 잘 짜인 책략 같은 느낌을 부여한다.

그러나 성 역할이 분명한 듯 보이는 인물의 행동은 여장남자의 느낌을 뛰어넘어 설명될 수 없다. 화면에서 보이는 요소와 전달 부분에서는 복잡함이 존재하나 성전환자의 구체성은 인물의 이야기를 통해 이미 소개됐다. 영상의 대부분 요소가 남/여로 구별된 몸이나 성의 유동성 또는 경직성과 맞닿아 혼란을 일으킨다.

아마도 영상에서 가장 강조된 부분은 양분된 여성과 남성의 활동을 뛰어넘은 공간을 정의하는 동시에 성 역할이 정해져 있는 신체에 대한 지식과 도구로써 활용되는 과학에 대한 방어일 것이다. 이러한 이슈는 중성 또는 간성이라 불리는 비 이분법적 체계 즉 개별 신체가 동시에 생물학적으로 여성성과 남성성 모두를 아우르는 것을 소개할 때 명시된 바 있으며 폭넓게 논평되어 왔다. 인물의 정체성은 우리가 과학과 생물학이 명료함의 공간 안에서 중점적으로 창조되는 것을 알거나 특정한 비규범적 주제에 대해서도 자세를 취할 수 있음을 받아들이는 데서 이해될 것이다.

Jessica Tsang, b.1984 and raised in Brunei, is a London-based artist who graduated from the Goldsmiths MFA in 2011 with distinction. Recent exhibitions include Concerning the Bodyguard at The Tetley, Leeds, Cash Nexus at AS Gallery, Krakow; Staged Relations at Impakt Festival, Utrecht; and Continuum at V22, London. Her film Erdös-Bacon Number was entered into Polish film archive, Ninateka. Recently she has been the recipient of a grant from the AHRC and has completed production residencies at EKWC, 's-Hertogenbosch and the Chinese Arts Centre, Manchester. Her films utilise the tools of both the documentarian and the sculptor carving out new stories within new filmic spaces. She is currently working on a project about an incident of mass hysteria at a girls' secondary school in Brunei. This film will examine both how these incidences in Brunei relate to global occurrences of mass hysteria, and, the state of belief in a country altering the structural relationship of religion and spirituality to law and governance.

또한, 가장 명확한 것은 몸에 대한 과학적 개념의 방어는 자연과 인공 사이에 명백히 나누어져 있는 반대 개념을 해체하는 것과도 맥락을 함께한다. '자연적'이고 '과학적'인 중성의 몸이 양분되지 않은 성 역할을 하는 몸의 본질적인 면을 지지한다면 표현되는 신체나 포괄하는 신체나 인공을 명시하는 신체 또한 성 역할을 전달할 것이다. 그렇다면 중성적 몸은 남성 여성의 범주를 넘어설 뿐 아니라 엄격하게 구분되거나 예상 밖의 새로운 성을 창조함으로써 젠더의 구분에 있어 새로운 장소를 제공하거나 지칭하는 의미로 사용될 것이다.

만약 이 공간이 생물학과 젠더 형성의 교차지점에 존재한다면 이것은 한편으로는 퀴어링의 범주에서 규정되어오던 트렌스젠더 (transgender)개념과 그와는 반대편에 존재하는 성전환 (transsexuality)개념의 충돌을 완화할 것이다. 다시 말해 영상에서 표현되는 중성적 몸은 비 이분법적 생물학의 범주를 긍정적으로 다루며 다양한 공간을 창조하는 동시에 새로운 성의 출현이나 도용의 가능성을 열어둔다. 이러한 결합은 과학적 방법론의 방어와 몸의 관계를 범주화시키는 사이에서 적극적으로 표현되며 성의 표현은 자연적인 것을 뛰어넘어선 것임을 보여준다.

작품의 제목을 봤을 때 우리는 화면을 가득 메우는 신체가 이런 공간을 제공한다는 것을 추측할 수 있다. 우리가 양극으로 나누어진 시스템상에서 '네' 또는 '아니오'로 대답할 때 '아마도'는 그 사이의 공간을 정의하는 동시에 불확실성 속에서 대안적 공간을 마련하는 가능성을 여는 단어가 될 것이다. 영상을 통해서는 눈에 보이는 신체의 생물학적 특성에 대해서는 들을 수 없을 뿐만 아니라 주인공의 여성성을 설명하는 표현에 대한 자연스러운 해결책도 찾을 수 없다. '아마도'라는 단어는 신체적으로 또는 성별로 나타난 우연을 상대할 수 있는 최적의 범위가 될 것이고 동시에 둘로 쪼개진 규범과는 딱 들어맞지 않는 몸과 정체성의 새로운 의미를 창조할 것이다.

1984년생으로 동남아시아 브루나이에서 자란 Jessica Tsang은 2011년 Goldsmiths 에서 미술 석사를 취득하고 런던을 기반으로 활동하는 작가다. 최근 영국의 Concerning Bodayguard at The Tetly 를 포함, 폴란드 Cash Nexus at AS Gallery, 네덜란드의 Impakt 페스티벌 연계 전시, 영국 런던 V22의 Continuum 에서 전시에 참여하였다. 그녀의 영화 Erdös-Bacon Number은 폴란드 필름 아카이브 Ninateka에 아카이빙되었다. 최근 그녀는 AHRC (예술 인문 연구 협회) 로부터 지원금을 지원받았고, EKWC (Europees Keramisch werkcentrum), 's-Hertogenbosch, 그리고 맨체스터에 위치한 중국아트센터에서 레지던시를 하였다. 그녀는 영화의 다큐멘터리 적, 기록적 기능과 새로운 영화적 공간들 안의 참신한 이야기를 발굴하고 조각하는 능력을 동시에 이용한다. 그녀는 브루나이 여중학교에서 발생한 대규모 히스테리 사건에 관한 프로젝트를 진행하고 있다. 이 영화는 전 세계적으로 발생하고 있는 집단 히스테리 사건들과 브루나이와 어떤 관련성을 맺고 있고, 어떠한 영향을 끼쳤는가를 연구한다. 동시에 이 영화는 종교와 영성의 구조적 관계를 법과 정부로 치환시키는 국가 안에서의 믿음의 상태에 대한 연구이기도 하다.

Jessica Tsang, *Yes, No, Maybe* (2014), stills from digital video

LEAH UCHITEL

By Leah Uchitel

Contemporary art tries to find new symbols, to invent new language, to construct new icons. I do something different, going quite to the opposite direction. I see the contemporary art as a reflection of the contemporary life, which demands from us to see a mixture of familiar images in quite unexpected conjunctions. The art always was a way of communication, but in past centuries, it abandoned more and more this function leaving it to the written word. I see the writing itself as a form of art. This way I turn to the past of the region I live in, using the traditional images taken from the Ancient Near East and turning them into the contemporary icons intimately interwoven into the contemporary way of life.

Using this background as a point of anchor, I try to extract these cultural icons in the form of visual symbols. My attempt creates tension between the universally recognizable symbols and their unconventional combination, challenging our ability in cultural identification. For example, I combine aesthetics of the Ancient Near East expressed primarily through the script consisted of visual symbols with the aesthetics of the human body, which is central for the Western art going back to the Ancient Greek roots. In today's increasingly globalized world, ethnic identities are gradually becoming blurred, and the humankind is challenged by the fear of loss of individuality. At this point, I began to use the image of the house as a symbol of stability, belonging to a certain place, the reality, which in many senses has collapsed in contemporary mobile world. This tension is not confined to the general collective self-definitions, but also includes personal identifications in such fields as gender and religion. In this search, I try to extract from the common pool of cultural ideas and images interacting in a hybrid fashion, their original components in order to reconnect their sequences.

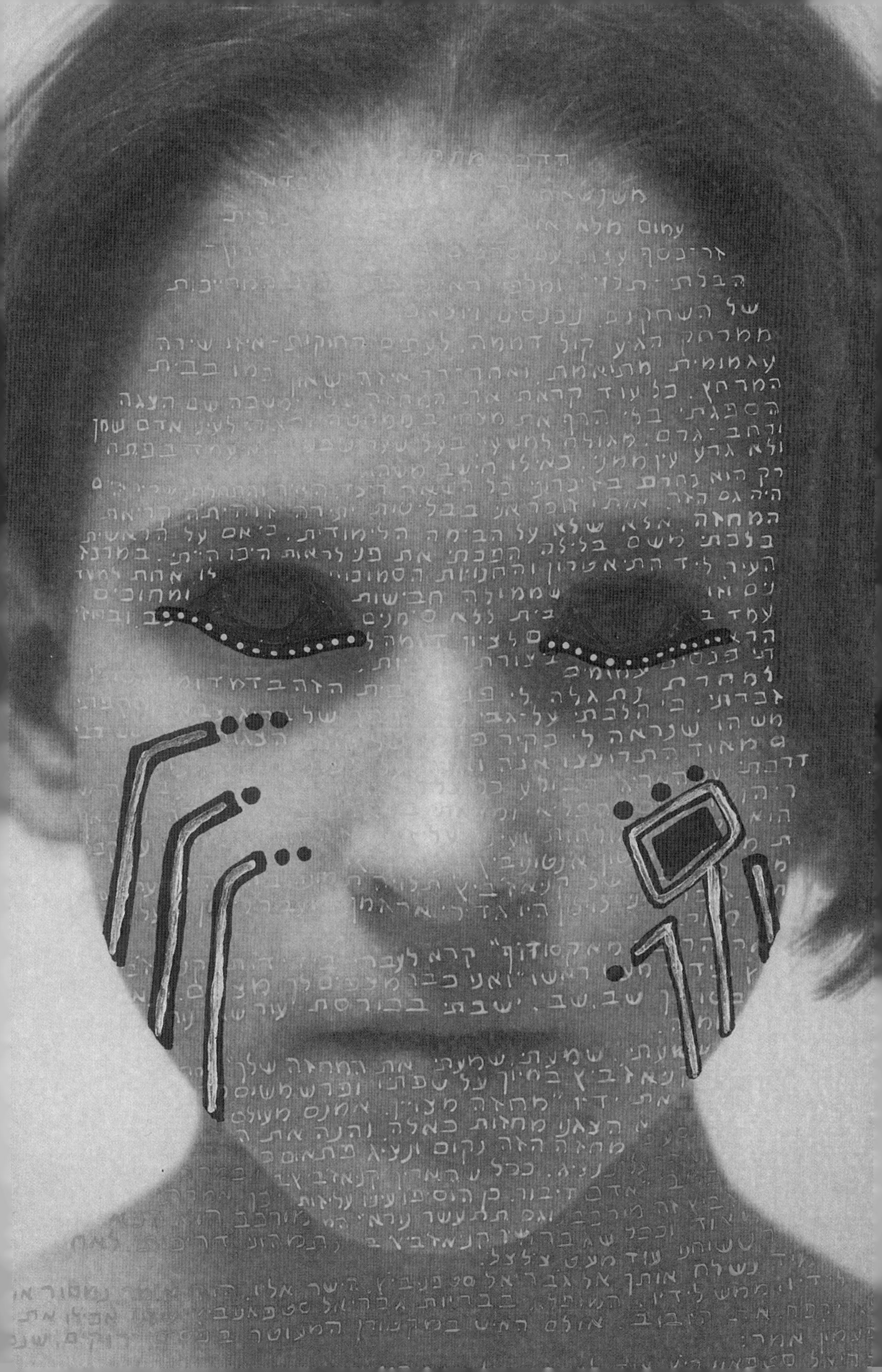

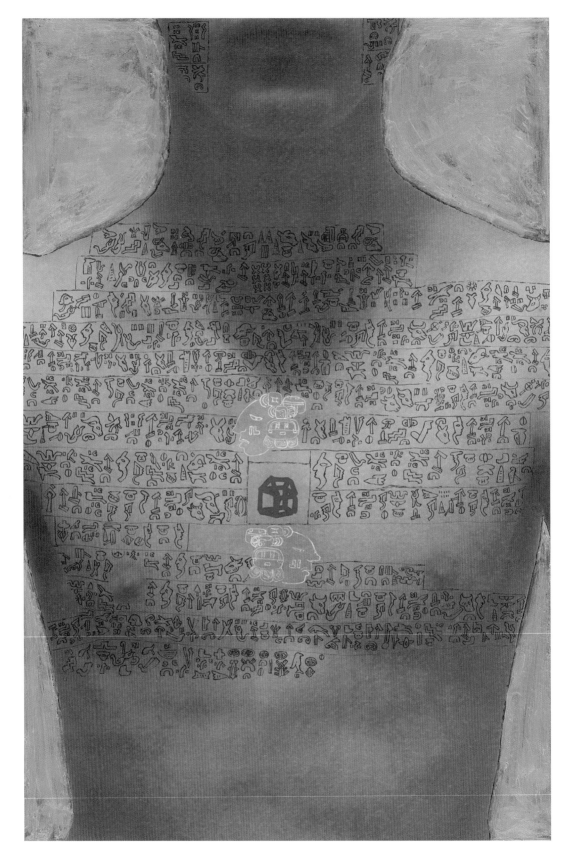

현대 예술은 새로운 상징을 발견하고, 새로운 언어를 발명하며, 새로운 아이콘을 만들어 낸다. 그러나 나는 이런 흐름의 반대 방향의 작업을 한다. 나는 현대예술이 동시대적 삶의 반영이라고 생각한다. 현대 예술은 우리가 예상치 못한 결합들 속에서 친밀한 이미지들을 볼 수 있도록 한다. 예술은 항상 소통의 방식이었다. 그러나 지난 몇 세기 동안 예술은 문자 언어에 소통의 역할을 떠넘긴 채 스스로 그 기능을 포기했다. 글쓰기는 그 자체로 예술의 한 형태이다. 나는 사는 지역의 고대 근동 전통 이미지를 우리 삶의 방식과 밀접하게 결합하여 있는 현대 아이콘으로 재생산해내는 작업을 하고 있다.

이것을 출발점으로 이러한 문화 아이콘을 시각적 상징물로 축출하려 했다. 보편적으로 인식되는 상징과 이의의 비관습적 조합을 통해 긴장을 유발하고, 우리의 문화적 인식력을 시험하고자 한다. 가령 나는 서양 미술의 근원이라 할 수 있는 고대 그리스의 인체 미학과 시각적 상징이 담긴 문자를 통해 표현된 고대 근동의 미학들을 결합하는 작업을 했다. 세계화가 가속화되는 현시점에서 민족적 정체성은 점차 희미해지고, 인류는 정체성 상실의 두려움에 직면했다. 현대의 유동적인 세계 속으로 붕괴하는 현실 속에서 나는 특정 장소에 속해 있는 집의 이미지를 안정성의 상징으로 사용하기 시작했다. 이러한 긴장감은 집단적 차원의 일반적인 정체성에만 국한된 것이 아니라 젠더나 종교 영역에서의 개인적 정체성도 포함한다. 이 연구들을 통해 문화적 아이디어와 하이브리드 패션 이미지가 차용한 원래 요소들을 추출하여 연속성을 재구축하고자 한다.

I am an Israeli artist who works mainly in Jerusalem, graduated from an art school in Jerusalem. Besides, I studied photography for two years and many times I combine photography at my artworks. In the past three years, I have deeply involved myself in visual aspects of the East Asia culture in general, and I have been particularly searching for its broader connection with other cultures. It led me to study Japanese language and calligraphy for two years, along with searching and returning to the aesthetics of the ancient Near East that was part of the area I live in today. The ancient world is a great inspiration for me. I am very interested in cultural symbols and their decomposition. Mostly I enjoy drawing their meaning into today's life and add to those ancient symbols, another layer.

나는 예루살렘의 예술 학교를 졸업한 후, 그곳에서 주로 활동하고 있는 이스라엘 예술가이다. 2년 동안 사진을 연구하면서 사진을 활용한 작업을 해왔다. 지난 3년 동안 나는 동아시아의 시각적 문화에 심취했다. 그중에서도 특히 동아시아 문화와 타문화와의 연계점 연구에 집중하고 있다. 고대 근동은 현재 내가 사는 지역의 한 부분이었다. 고대 근동의 미학으로 돌아가 그것을 연구하기 위해 지난 2년 동안 일본어와 서예를 공부했다. 고대 사회는 내 영감의 원천이라고 할 수 있다. 나는 문화적 상징들과 그것들의 해체에 관심이 있다. 나는 주로 현대의 삶 속에 침투해 있는 문화적 상징들의 의미를 그린다. 그리고 그 위에 고대의 상징들이라는 또 다른 겹을 입힌다.

JEFFREY YIP

Light Tunnel explores new terrain in an alien environment. Light traverses up and down this space in unison of sound to only leave its shadow behind. Light cannot exist without darkness just as well as the perception of darkness is only realized through light. *Light Tunnel* is meant to allow spectators to experience light and shadow in space to recontextualize the notion of how we experience them.

Rabbit Hole is a tessellated array of pyramids in a spiral formation. Light travels along this pyramidal landscape revealing a pathway into an unknown realm. Synthesized sounds unite with light bringing life to this transdimensional space. Rabbit Hole invites viewers to imagine an environment not familiar to our everyday lives.

*빛의 터널*은 낯선 환경 안에서의 새로운 지형을 탐구한다. 빛은 그림자를 드리우며 이 소리와 일치된 공간을 위아래로 횡단한다. 어둠을 빛을 통해서만 인지할 수 있듯이 빛은 어둠이 없다면 존재할 수 없다. *빛의 터널*에서 관람객은 새롭게 맥락화된 공간 안에서 빛과 어둠을 경험한다.

*토끼 굴*은 피라미드 형태의 모자이크 나선형으로 배열한 것이다. 빛은 보이지 않는 영역으로 길을 밝히면서 이 피라미드형 풍경을 관통한다. 합성된 음향과 빛은 결합하며 초월적 공간을 형성한다. *토끼 굴*은 관람객을 일상적이지 않은 초월적 공간으로 초대한다.

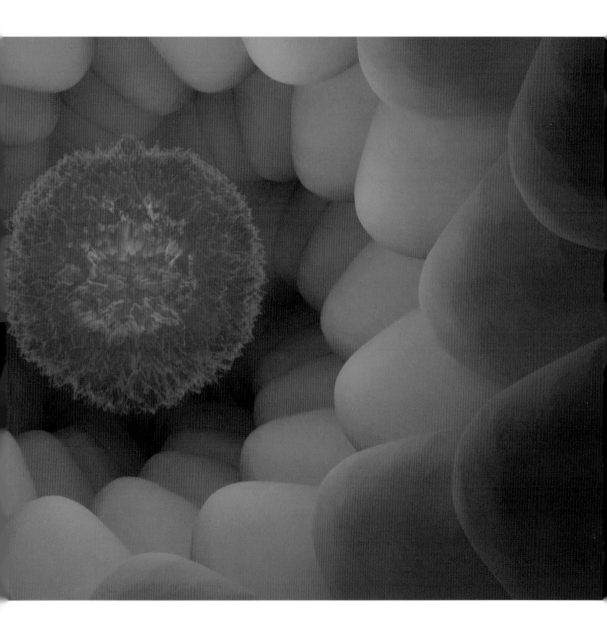

Jeffrey Yip, *Light Tunnel* (2017), still from digital video

Jeffrey Yip is a new media artist in Oakland California. Highly interested in the intersection of art and technology, he creates environments, often utilizing digital media to enhance the overall experience by integrating visualizations in unison with sound. One area of focus currently in his practice is projection mapping. This technique allows Jeffrey to combine the digital world with the physical through light, sound and sculpture. Animation is layered on top of his geometric sculptures, and then joined with organic and synthesized sound to create a symbiosis of the various mediums.

Jeffrey Yip은 캘리포니아 오클랜드를 기반으로 활동하는 뉴 미디어 아티스트이다. 예술과 기술의 상호작용에 큰 관심을 두고 있는 Jeffrey는 경험 전반을 향상해줄 수 있는 환경을 조성하기 위해 음향과 영상을 결합한다. 그가 현재 집중하고 있는 작업은 프로젝션 맵핑이다. Jeffrey는 프로젝션 맵핑으로 빛과 음향, 조각을 이용해 실제와 디지털 세계를 결합한다. 애니메이션은 그의 기하학적인 조각들 위에 중첩되고, 유기적 합성 사운드가 함께 다양한 미디어를 아우른다.

Jeffrey Yip, *Rabbit Hole* (2017), still from digital video

TAYLOR YOCOM

Eating lunch
Reading a book.
In public.
&by myself.

I happen to be a woman.
Someone approaches who
Happens to be a man

He wants to talk.
He wants to tell me this inter-
esting thing that i should be so
interested in
On and on and on and on
He doesn't even ask how i am
Just on and on and on

I look up
Nod
Give him a smile
Because that's what i'm sup-
posed to do, right?

Because that's nice, right?

But what is nice?
Is niceness a true action?
Or is it a performative reaction
to a situation?
Why am i supposed to be "nice"
anyways?

is it because i was taught to be
lady like from a young age?
Is it because showing that i'm
uncomfortable isn't nice?
Because i'm expected to carry
myself with an air of naivety and
the ability to be impressed at
the drop of a hat?

Smile and nod
Smile and nod

Oh wow!
No way!

Cool!
Uh huh!

He keeps going
I look at my book
I look back up
This conversation sure is one
sided

Oh wow!
No way!
Cool!
Uh huh!

Why do we feign interest when
we feel like we're trapped?
Why do we follow this same
script?
Oh wow!
No way!
Cool!
Uh huh!

He said that?
I want to get up

Oh wow!

God, leave me alone.

No way!

I am saying this because I feel
like I have to.

Cool!

This is so uncomfortable

Uh huh!

This is practically a performance

Oh wow!

Taylor Yocom, *Conversation Captivity!* (2016), stills from digital video

WOW

점심 먹고
독서 하기.
밖에서.
나 혼자서.

나는 어쩌다 보니 여자이다.
어떤 사람이 다가오는데
어쩌다 보니 남자

그는 말하고 싶어 해.
그는 내가 재미있어야만 하는 재미있는 뭔가에 대해 말해
계속 계속 계속
내가 어떻게 받아들이는지 생각도 않고
그저 계속 계속 계속

내가 그를 올려보고
끄덕이고
미소도 지어주고
그게 내가 해야 할 일이잖아, 그렇지?

그게 착한 거니까, 그렇지?

뭐가 착한 거야?
착하게 행동하는 것에 진심이 담겨 있을까?
아니면 상황에 반응하는 기계적 행동일까?
왜 내가 "착하게" 행동해야만 하지?

내가 어릴 때부터 숙녀가 되는 법을 배웠기 때문일까?
내가 불편하다는 걸 보여주는 게 착하지 않기 때문인가?
내게 순진하고 쉽게 감동하기를 기대해서일까?

웃고 끄덕이고
웃고 끄덕여

와 대박!
말도 안 돼!
멋지다!
으응!

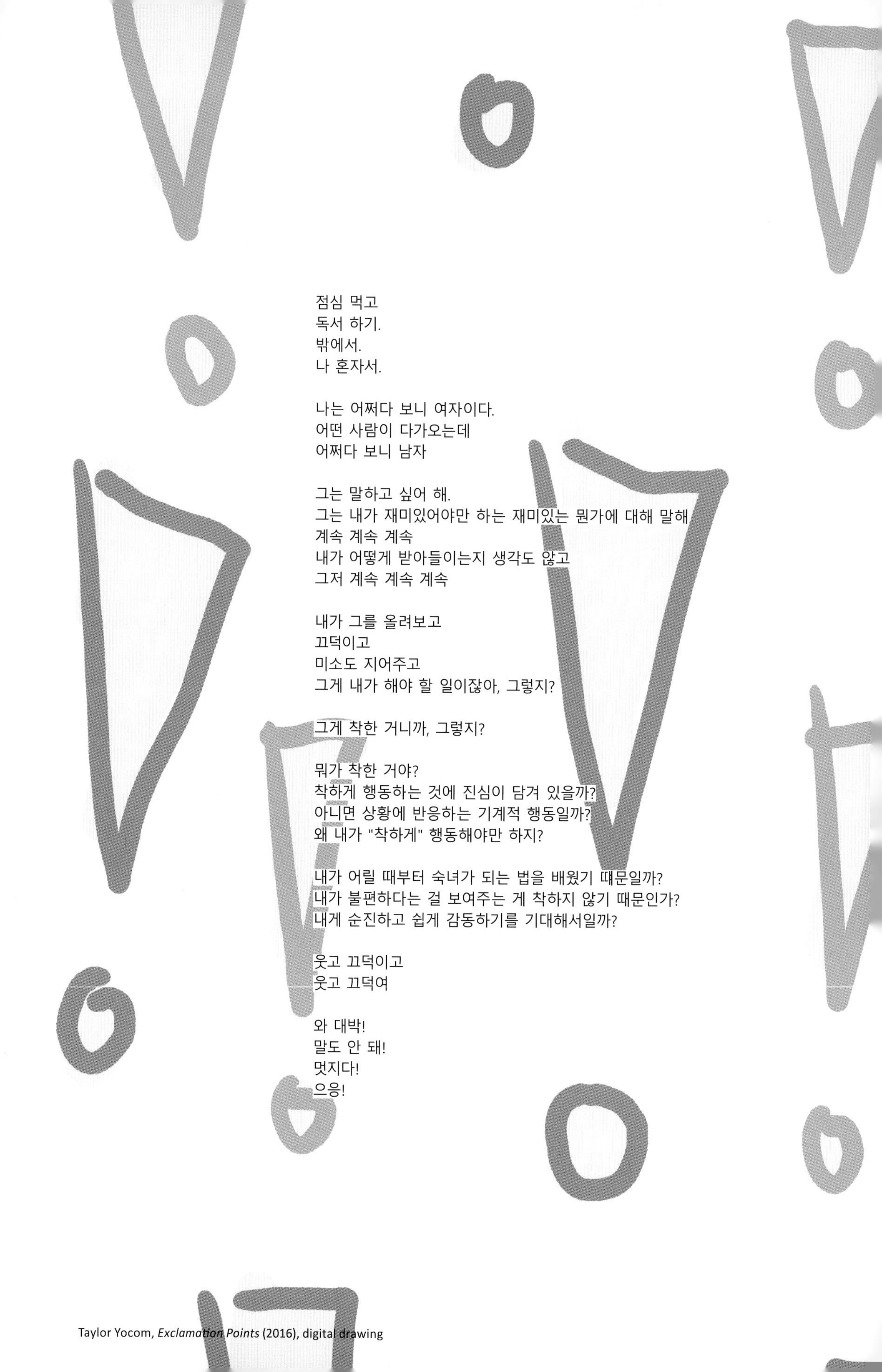

Taylor Yocom, *Exclamation Points* (2016), digital drawing

그는 계속 떠들고
내 시선을 책으로 갔다
다시 올려다보고
이 대화는 당연히 일방적이지

와 대박!
말도 안 돼!
멋지다!
으응!

난감한 상황에 처할 때 왜 우린 관심 있
는 척할까?
왜 이 지루한 반응을 반복할까?
와 대박!
말도 안 돼!
멋지다!
으응!

걔가 그랬다고?
그냥 일어나고 싶어

와 대박!

제발 나 좀 내버려 둬

말도 안돼!

이렇게 말하는 건 그냥 의무감 때문
이야.

멋지다!

이건 너무 불편해

저런!

이 정도면 퍼모먼스라고 해야지

와 대박!

Taylor Yocom (BFA Photography, University of Iowa 2015) uses mixed media, installation, video, and photography to explore the gender performativity of "female niceness." Her work has been exhibited regionally and nationally and she is a Bustle Upstarts award recipient. Her striking photo series, Guarded, has appeared internationally in renowned publications such as Buzzfeed, USA Today, and the US and UK versions of the Huffington Post. She is currently working towards her MFA in Visual Art in Washington University in St. Louis's Sam Fox School of Design and Visual Arts.

Taylor Yocom 2015년 아이오와 대학 사진학 학사를 취득 후 혼합 매체, 설치, 비디오 및 사진을 이용해 "착한 여자"를 주제로 작업한다. 그녀의 작품은 전국적으로 전시되었고 Bustle Upstarts 상을 받았다. 그녀의 파격적인 사진 시리즈 Guarded는 Buzzfeed, US Tday 및 미국과 영국 버전의 허핑턴 포스트와 같은 유명한 출판물에서 국제적으로 소개되었다. 현재 그녀는 워싱턴 대학에서 미술 석사 과정에 있다.

LILIYA ZALEVSKAYA

"The absurdity of reality demands a form which dismantles the realistic facade"
-Adorno

Though my work comes out of a specific idea, it does not seek to communicate a particular or coherent position, but rather to offer an alternate way of approaching that idea from three different points of view, creating a sense of wonder. It is this method of inquiry that I am interested in. The work is an artifact of a thought process, evoking notions of absurdity. The Absurd as defined in philosophical discourse is the human search for meaning and the inability to find any. Therefore, when one is faced with a meaningless universe, there are three options to resolve the dilemma. According to absurdist philosophy the first option, not very practical, is suicide. The second is spiritual or religious transcendence, believing in the reality beyond the absurd. And, the third solution is the acceptance and even the embrace of the absurd. The three possible positions: of escape, transcendence, and acceptance, are used as the points of departure from which I approach the subject matter in a particular piece.

The concept of nonsensical, non-linear plots, wordplay, parody and dismissal of realism explored in visual art, literature and cinema inform my work. Particularly, I am drawn to literary works of writers such as Gogol, Kafkaand Bulgakov. Narratives where characters are faced with a strange and mysterious force that can be understood as the existential concept of the Absurd.

Working with video allows me to incorporate time, space and my own body as tools. Through the manipulation of time and space I can alter the perception of reality by imposing the fantastic. The body serves as a medium to express both the fantastic and the real. In my current work, I investigate two structures: one focuses on the space in which the body exists; the other, focuses on the experience of living as a search for understanding.

In The Three Series, the characters are a manifestation of a single identity, dealing with the experience of the world approached from the three positions: escape, transcendence and acceptance. The characters are distinguished by their appearance and each loosely represent a point of view according to absurdist philosophy. The clown character has accepted the absurd, and therefore directly manifest it. She is silent and mostly seeks meaning in play and reflection on what is experienced through creation. The studious character is concerned with fundamental problems of matters such as existence, knowledge, values and reason, eventually deciding that the suicide is the ultimate solution. The character wearing make-up and a skirt is seeking transcendence. She does not necessarily believe in the reality beyond the absurd, but like a rebellious teenager seeks comparable worldly experiences.

The fantastic emerges from anxiety caused by the search for understanding and initiates a break with everyday and routine activities. The reasonable now seems irrational and the familiar begins to appear strange. Thus, we see a gap between thought and reality. This incomprehensible gap between real and fantastic Idenote as Absurdity. Absurdity is further heightened by the want to construct a linear narrative where there is not one. The characters are not responsible and have no remedy for this situation, but merely respond according to their own perspective. I want the viewer to be intrigued by the imagery and yet be frustrated by the absurdity of the content.

My work is not about finding a specific solution but about the process of looking for meaning through play. I want to offer the viewer an escape from logical, transforming the mundane into wondrous.

Liliya Zalevskaya, *The Golden Fish*, still from digital video

"현실의 부조리는 현실적 허울을 일그러뜨릴 수 있는 양식을 요구한다"

- 아도르노

내 작업은 구체적인 아이디어에서 시작되기는 하지만 어떤 특정 요소나 일관적 상태에 관해서만 이야기하고자 하는 것은 아니다. 그것보다는 세 가지의 다른 관점에서 보는 대안적 방법을 제시하며 경이로운 감각을 창조하고자 한다. 그러니까 나는 의문을 만들어내는 방식에 관심이 있는 것이다. 내가 만든 작품은 내 생각의 과정이 드러나는 인공물이며 불합리성의 이미지를 떠올리게 만든다. 철학적으로 명시되는 부조리란 개인이 의미를 찾고자 노력하나 결국 어떤 것도 찾지 못하게 된다는 무능력에 대한 이야기이다. 그러므로 한 사람이 의미 없는 우주와 맞딱뜨린다고 가정하면 거기엔 딜레마를 해결할 수 있는 세 가지 방법이 있다. 부조리 철학에 따르자면 매우 실용적이라 말할 수는 없지만, 첫 번째 방법은 자살이 될 것이다. 두 번째 방법은 현실은 불합리성의 우위에 있다고 믿는 정신적 또는 종교적 초월성을 들 수 있다. 그리고 세 번째 해결책은 현실의 부조리를 받아들이거나 심지어 포용하는 방법이 될 것이다. 세 가지의 가능한 해결 방법들, 즉 도망치거나, 초월하거나, 순응하는 모습들은 내가 특정 작업에서 주제를 제시할 때 사용하는 출발점이 된다.

시각 예술, 문학, 그리고 영화에서 사용되는 터무니 없거나 순차적이지 않은 이야기 구성들 그리고 말장난이나 패러디 사실주의를 뭉개는 개념들이 내 작업에 영향을 미친다. 특별히 Gogol, Kafka, Bulgakov 의 문학 작품들에 이끌렸다. 작중 인물들이 이상하면서도 알 수 없는 힘들과 대면하는 장면들을 통해서 부조리의 존재론적 개념을 이해할 수 있었다.

매체로서의 비디오는 시간과 공간 그리고 내 몸을 도구로 사용할 수 있게 해 주었다. 시공간을 조작함으로써 환상들을 동원해 현실에 대한 개념을 바꿀 수 있었다. 몸은 환상과 현실 두 요소를 모두 표현하는 도구로 사용되었다. 최근작에서는 두 가지 구성을 탐구 중이다. 하나는 몸이 존재하는 공간에 대한 탐구이며 다른 하나는 삶의 경험이라는 것이 이해를 찾아 나가는 과정이라는 것에 대해 초점을 맞추고 있다.

The Three Series에서 인물들은 개별 정체성을 표현하며 앞서 말한 세 가지의 자세(도망, 초월, 받아들임)를 통해 세상을 경험한다. 부조리 철학에 따르자면 인물들은 그들의 외형적 특징으로도 구별되며 각각은 그 관점들을 느슨하게나마 표현한다. 광대는 불합리성을 받아들이며 즉각적으로 반응한다. 그녀는 조용하며 대부분 시간은 자신의 역할에서 의미를 찾거나 창작행위를 통한 경험을 숙고한다. 학구적인 인물은 존재나 지식 가치 등의 근본적 문제들을 고뇌하며 끝내 자살이 최종 해결책이 될 것이라 결정한다. 화장하고 치마를 입은 인물은 초월을 찾는다. 그녀는 불합리성을 넘어선 현실을 그다지 신뢰하지 않으나 반항적 십 대 같은 세속적 경험을 추구한다.

환상은 이해하고자 하는 노력에서 오는 불안으로부터 야기되며 반복되는 일상과 일과에 균열을 일으킨다. 합리성은 이제 비이성적으로 보이며 친숙한 것들은 이상하게 보이기 시작한다. 따라서 우리는 생각과 현실 사이의 격차를 보게 된다. 현실과 환상의 이해할 수 없는 틈을 나는 부조리라 표현한다. 부조리는 하나의 결말로 존재하지 않는 이야기를 순차적으로 나열하고자 하는 요구 때문에 더욱 심화한다. 화면 속의 등장인물들은 자신이 처한 환경 속에서 해결책이 없을 뿐만 아니라 그 상황을 초래한 책임 또한 지지 않고 있으며 겨우 자신들의 관점에 따라 반응하고 있을 뿐이다. 나는 관객들이 이러한 이미지들에 이끌리기를 바라면서도 한편으로는 부조리한 요소들에 대해 절망하기를 원한다.

내 작업은 구체적 해결책을 찾고자 하는 것이 아니라 재생되는 화면을 통해 의미를 찾아 나가는 과정이다. 나는 관객들에게 논리에서 벗어나 일상적인 것을 경이로운 것으로 바꾸는 경험을 제공하고자 한다.

Liliya Zalevskaya was born in Kiev, Ukraine. As a young teenager, her family immigrated to America, as the Soviet Union fell apart. This continues to inform her interest in how social structures are perceived versus how they are experienced by the individuals living within them. In essence the work is the artifact of play, through which she interrogates the roles as a director, actor, and editor in the construction of a fantasy that questions reality. Liliya often collaborates with her partner artist David Scott Sackett. Liliya received a BFA in Printmaking from the University of North Carolina at Charlotte and an MFA in Digital Media from the University of North Carolina at Greensboro.

Liliya Zalevkya는 우크라이나의 키예프라는 도시에서 태어났다. 그녀가 청소년기에 소련이 붕괴함에 따라 미국으로 이민을 했다. 개인의 삶 속에서 사회적 구조가 어떻게 받아들여 지는지는 지속해서 그녀의 주된 관심사였다. 본질적으로 작품은 희극의 인위적 구조에 기반을 둔다. 현실에 대한 의문을 제기하는 환상을 구축하며 그녀는 감독과 배우, 편집자의 역할에 질문을 던진다. Liliya 는 그녀의 파트너 David Scott Sackett 과 종종 공동 작업을 한다. Liliya는 샬럿의 노스캐롤라이나 대학에서 판화 학사를 취득했으며, 그린즈버러의 노스캐롤라이나 대학에서 디지털 미디어 전공으로

Liliya Zalevskaya, *The Golden Fish*, still from digital video